ON THE ROAD TO RESURRECTION

JACK McARDLE SS CC

On the Road to Resurrection

DAILY REFLECTIONS FOR LENT

THE COLUMBA PRESS
DUBLIN 2004

THE COLUMBA PRESS
55A Spruce Avenue, Stillorgan Industrial Park,
Blackrock, Co Dublin

First edition 2004
Cover by Bill Bolger
Origination by
The Columba Press
Printed in Ireland by
ColourBooks Ltd, Dublin

ISBN 1 85607 467 6

CONTENTS

Introduction

I wrote a book called *Stepping Stones To Bethlehem*, which were daily reflections for Advent. The positive response to that book has encouraged me to offer *On The Road To Resurrection* as daily reflections for Lent. I don't know about you, but it certainly helps me to have some sort of daily road-map to guide me through those special times, that, on my own, I might aimlessly wander through, without much thought or reflection. I need something that will enable me keep focused, to be alert, and to prepare as best I can for the moment of grace that is offered.

The evolution of this book was quite interesting, because I began with no prepared menu, or hidden agenda. I opened my heart to the Spirit, and I tried to be faithful to where I was being guided. This lead me to begin each reflection with scripture quotations, as if I were anxious to give the Lord the first word, rather than anything I might have to say. This approach was topped off, when I came to a concluding prayer, by presenting some verses from the psalms. The psalms were prayers that Jesus himself prayed, and it's not possible to improve on that. Many of us may not be very familiar with the psalms as prayers but, hopefully, after reading each reflection, the words of each psalm may have more meaning for us.

The titles I chose for each reflection were completely spontaneous and instinctual. I could have set out to select themes that had some order or sequence, but I felt that this could become very artificial and construed. As it happened, I just chose the first word that came to mind, whether it encapsulated the core of that day or not. The Spirit works in extraordinary ways and, like the seagull, I love to 'ride the wind' and, opening my wings, I let the wind do the work. I enjoyed this process, because it gave me the freedom to 'go with the flow', and let the process unfold.

I made a very deliberate decision to avoid being specific in what I might do each day, in response to the reflection. We are all so different, and each of us has the capacity to hear and to respond to things in different ways. I felt that someone who had gone to the trouble of getting this book in the first place, would also have the capacity to bring a personal response to what was offered. My experience has taught me to respect the other, and to allow for the variety of possibilities within the hearts of each of us. It would be a very interesting experiment to 'round up' the readers, and compare notes on how each of us responded to the invitation that was offered! The collage of our responses could possibly make up a complete response. None of us has a monopoly on God, and this book is offered in the knowledge that each reader is different, each reception of the word will be different and, therefore, each response will be different.

I myself have gained immensely from writing these reflections. I have written for myself, in that I wrote as if I were the only one who was ever going to read them. The fact that they might be a source of help and blessing to others is, indeed, a bonus, a privilege, and something for which I am deeply grateful. Once again, as with other books, I pray that you, the reader, may be blessed in the reading, just as I have been blessed in the writing.

ASH WEDNESDAY

Sackcloth and Ashes

'On the twenty-fourth day of that same month, the Israelites assembled to fast. They put on sackcloth and sprinkled dust upon their heads. The race of Israel separated themselves from all foreigners; they stood and confessed their sins and those of their fathers. They stood up in their place and read from the Book of the Law of Yahweh, their God, for another three hours. For another three hours, they confessed their sins, and bowed before Yahweh, their God.' (Neh 9:1-3) 'I, Daniel, thought about the number of years, according to the scriptures, before Jerusalem should be left in ruins. Yahweh spoke of seventy years to the prophet Jeremiah. I turned to the Lord and begged him. I pleaded with prayers and fasting. I did penance, I put on sackcloth, and sat on an ash heap.' (Dan 9:2-3) 'On the day Jonah entered the city, he shouted to the crowds: "Forty days from now Nineveh will be destroyed." The people of Nineveh believed God's message, and from the greatest to the least, they decided to go without food, and wear sackcloth to show their sorrow. When the king of Nineveh heard what Jonah was saying, he stepped down from his throne, and took off his loyal robes. He dressed himself in sackcloth, and sat on a heap of ashes … He sent a decree around the city: "Everyone is required to wear sackcloth, and pray earnestly to God. Everyone must turn from their evil ways, and stop all their violence. Who can tell? Perhaps even yet God will have pity on us, and hold back his fierce anger from destroying us".' (Jonah 3:4-9)

I have found seventeen other references in the Old Testament to the use of ashes and sackcloth as a token of repentance, and sorrow for sin. Sackcloth preceded the coffin as a way of burial. To wear sackcloth was a symbol of our mortality. Ashes were also a sign of death, being all that is left when something is completely destroyed by fire. We begin this season of Lent by being brought face to face with our own frailty and mortality, and we end it with Jesus overcoming death, and obtaining for us the wonderful gift of immortality.

To do

The reading for today paints in the background of the history of God's people, when it came to repentance, and turning back to him. At least that was some external sign, if properly understood. What I suggest today is that we try to get a feel for the symbolism of wearing sackcloth and ashes. Because these daily reflections will lead us to the glory of resurrection, it is good to be deeply aware of just how human, mortal, frail, and fragile we really are. If you have had a chance to get ashes on your forehead today, give some serious and sincere thinking about the significance of that act.

To say

Psalm 6

O Lord, do not rebuke me in your anger, or discipline me in your rage.

Have compassion on me, Lord, for I am weak. Heal me, Lord, for my body is in agony.

I am sick at heart. How long, O Lord, will you restore me?

Return, O Lord, and rescue me. Save me because of your unfailing love.
For in death, who remembers you? Who can praise you from the grave?
I am worn out from sobbing. Every night tears drench my bed, my pillow is wet with weeping.
O God, be merciful to me, a sinner.

THURSDAY AFTER ASH WEDNESDAY

Calling All Sinners

'If we say we have no sin, we are only fooling ourselves, and refusing to accept the truth. But if we confess our sins to him, he is faithful and just to forgive us, and to cleanse us of every wrong. If we claim we have not sinned, we are calling God a liar, and showing that his word is not in our hearts.' (1 Jn 1:8-9) 'Sin whispers to the wicked, deep within their hearts. They have no fear of God to restrain them. In their blind conceit, they cannot see how wicked they really are.' (Ps 36:1-2) 'Return, O Israel, to the Lord your God, for your sins have brought you down. Bring your petitions, and return to the Lord. Say to him "Forgive all our sins, and graciously receive us, so that we may offer you the sacrifice of praise".' (Hos 14:1-2) I began this chapter with some random quotes from the Old Testament, before looking at, and listening to what Jesus has to say about sin, repentance and conversion (which we will begin with tomorrow). I have to make very arbitrary choices in selecting a quotation, because there are so many of them spoken through the mouths of the prophets. Since the Fall in the Garden, God has always been calling his people to come back to him. I have chosen a few of the many calls of God in the Old Testament, inviting his people back to the Garden. I will let the words speak for themselves, because there is no way that I could add any power to a word that is spoken by God. As you read his words, and reflect on them, I will suggest something very simple to do today, and provide you with a short prayer to help launch you into the day. Naturally, we will continue with more of the same for at least this first week in Lent.

To do

Select one of the passages from this reflection, write it on a piece of paper, and carry it on your person throughout the day. Find out for yourself how aware you are of having that paper, what is written on it, and what it means to you.

To say

Psalm 51

Have mercy on me, O God, because of your unfailing love.
Because of your great compassion, blot out the stain of my sins.
Wash me clean from my guilt, purify me from my sin.
For I recognise my shameful deeds – they haunt me day and night.
Against you, and you alone, have I sinned;
I have done what is evil in your sight.

Purify me from my sins, and I will be clean;
Wash me, and I will be whiter than snow.

Don't keep looking at my sins.
Remove the stain of my guilt.
Create in me a clean heart, O God.
Renew a right spirit within me.

FRIDAY AFTER ASH WEDNESDAY

What does Jesus Say?

'Healthy people don't need a doctor – sick people do. I have come to call sinners to turn from their sins, not to spend my time with those who think they are good enough.' (Lk 5:31-32) 'Turn away from your sins, because the kingdom of heaven is near.' (Mt 4:17) Defending a public sinner, Jesus said 'This is why, I tell you, her sins, her many sins, have been forgiven her because she loved much' ... Then turning to the woman he said 'Your sins are forgiven.' (Lk 7:47-48) 'I tell you there will be more rejoicing in heaven over one repentant sinner than over ninety-nine upright who do not need to repent.' (Lk 15:7) 'If I had not come to tell them, they would have no sin, but now they have no excuse for their sin ... If I had not done among them what no one else has ever done, they would have no sin.' (Jn 15:22, 24) 'They are wrong about sin because they do not believe in me.' (Jn 16:9) 'If you forgive people's sins they are forgiven.' (Jn 20:23)

John the Baptist prepared the way for Jesus. 'His message was "Turn from your sins and return to God, because the kingdom of heaven is near".' (Mt 3:2) 'People from Jerusalem, and from every section of Judea, and from all over the Jordan Valley went out to the wilderness to hear him speak. And when they confessed their sins, he baptised them in the Jordan river.' (Mt 3:5-6) 'The next day John saw Jesus coming toward him and said "Look! There is the Lamb of God who takes away the sin of the world. He is the one I was talking about when I said

'Soon a man is coming who is greater than I am, for he existed long before I did'."' (Jn 1:29-30)

Jesus was very insistent that he came in search of sinners, because it was not his Father's will that any of his children be lost. Of all the people he met, it is interesting to see that he felt completely at ease with sinners, and they certainly found a genuine and compassionate heart in him.

To do

More or less a repeat of yesterday! Pick a quotation that strikes you and gives you food for thought; write it on a piece of paper, and carry it on your person all day. If you work at a desk, you could place it in front of you so that your attention is drawn to it from time to time. Remember the word is from Jesus, so it has a power of its own, so that you will be lead beyond the words to the truth they contain.

To say

Psalm 23

The Lord is my shepherd, I shall not want.
He makes me lie down in green pastures, he leads me beside the still waters.
He restores my soul.
He guide me through the path of righteousness, for his name sake.
Although I walk through the valley of the shadow of death, I fear no evil,
For you are beside me. Your rod and your staff are there to comfort me.

SATURDAY AFTER ASH WEDNESDAY

Repentance

'Yahweh, the God of Israel, says this: "The warnings of this book shall not reach you, for your heart has been touched, and you have done penance in the sight of Yahweh, when you heard what I had said against this place".' (2 Kgs 22:18-19) 'If they sin against you – for there is no one who does not sin – and you are angry with them, and deliver them to the enemy....If they come to themselves and repent, saying "We have sinned, we confess how sinful and wicked we have been", please hear their prayer, and forgive your people the sins they have committed against you.' (2 Chron 6:36-39) 'Repent then, and turn to God, so that he may forgive you.' (Acts 3:19) When recovering alcoholics attend an AA meeting, there are simple slogans placed around the room to remind them of basic truths. One of them is '*Think, think, think.*' We speak of someone being in a pensive mood, meaning that the person is deep in thought. Lent is a time when we are asked to *think* again about our life, and how we are living it. Many of our sins and failings come from sheer thoughtlessness, when we act without giving any thought to the consequences of our actions. A thoughtful person is usually kind, and considerate of others.

When the television first arrived in our living rooms, before we had aerials on the chimney, or satellite dishes on the side of our houses, we had what we called 'rabbits' ears', or antennae, on our TV sets. With these, we were able to pick up local stations, which was all that was available at the time. To think is to have such antennae on our heads, so that we can pick up the vibes coming from those around us. We are aware if someone is hurting, or if what we said or did has caused them hurt. The sensitive person is a thinking person, and is in a constant state of repentance. This enables such people to be aware when they're wrong, and they have the ability to admit it. Lent is a time when we sharpen our sensitivities, and take responsibility for our words and actions.

To do

Select a particular time and situation today when you become as fully alert as you can to what is happening around you. Think of that antenna on your head, and become as aware as you can of what you are doing, how you're doing it, and what or who is being effected by what you do. Heighten the level of your sensitivity, whether that involves listening, speaking, or being as present as you can to someone around you, or to some task at hand. *Live* that moment with deliberate awareness, and take full responsibility for how you use that time.

To say

Psalm 1

Oh, the joy of those who do not follow the advice of the wicked,
Or stand around with sinners, or join in with scoffers.
They delight in doing everything the Lord wants;
Day and night they think about his laws.
They are like trees planted along the riverbank,
Bearing fruit each season without fail.
Their leaves never wither,
And in all they do, they prosper.

FIRST SUNDAY OF LENT

Truth

'Joshua then said to him: "My son, confess the truth before Yahweh, the God of Israel, and render him praise. Tell me what you have done, without hiding anything." Achan answered: "It is true that I have sinned against Yahweh. This is what I have done ..."' (Josh 7:19-20) 'An honest witness tells the truth; a false witness tells lies. Truth stands the test of time; lies are soon exposed.' (Prov 12:17, 19) 'I have much to say about you, and much to condemn; but the One who sent me is truthful, and everything I learned from him, I proclaim to the world.' (Jn 8:26) 'When he, the Spirit of truth comes, he will guide you into the whole truth.' (Jn 16:13) Original sin was the result of a lie, brought about by Satan, the father of lies. All sin is a lie, because it can never deliver what it promises, and it seriously damages our integrity and worth as people. Each one of us has an inbuilt barometer, which we call 'conscience', and it serves as a lie detector. Quite a lot of publicity was given recently to the arrest and conviction of a double child murderer in England. We were shown films of the interviews with him in the police station, and experts pointed out how his whole demeanour and manner conveyed the fact that he was lying. The liar has to have a good memory!

I can speak a lie, or live a lie. We sometimes hear of someone 'being economical with the truth', which is another way of saying that the person is telling the truth, but not the whole truth. That is why the oath taken in a court of law speaks about 'telling the truth, the whole truth, and nothing but the truth'. We speak about 'telling the truth to shame the devil', because God's Spirit is a Spirit of truth, and deceit and lies are not of God. There is a wonderful freedom in the truth. Ask any recovering alcoholic about the freedom that follows when one faces up to the truth. Jesus tells us 'You will be my true disciples if you keep my word. Then you will know the truth, and the truth will set you free.' (Jn 8:31-32)

To do

When we die, we will stand before God, exactly as we are. No more hiding, excusing, denying, pretending. The canvas of our lives will be opened out fully before the Lord. I suggest that you do not wait till you die for this to happen. You can do that this very day. Find a quiet moment, when you can open out the canvas of your life before God … out … out … out to the very edges. What do you think God will see? We are not saints, and I'm not speaking of appearing spotless before him. What I suggest you do is imagine what deceit and lies may appear on that canvas. The Spirit of Truth will reveal all of that to me any day I am prepared to know.

To say

Psalm 119

Give me your unfailing love, O Lord, your salvation as you have promised.

Strengthened by my trust in your word, I can answer my enemy's reproach.

Take not the word of truth from my mouth, for I would also lose my hope in your word.

May I always keep your word for ever and ever; I shall walk in freedom, having sought out your laws.

I will proclaim your word before people, and I will not be confused or ashamed.

For I delight in your word. I revere your word, which I hold dear; and I meditate on your commandments.

FIRST MONDAY OF LENT

Broken

'My heart breaks when I remember the past. Why are you so downcast, my soul, why so troubled within me? I say to God, my rock, "Why have you forgotten me? Why do I go about mourning, harassed and oppressed by my enemy?"' (Ps 42:4, 6, 10) 'Therefore the Holy One of Israel says, "Because you despise this word, this guilt of yours will be like a breach on a high wall, cracked and bulging, ready to fall. It will be like the breaking of a potter's vessel, smashed so ruthlessly that among its fragments not one shard remains big enough to scoop cinder out of the hearth, or ladle water out of the cistern".' (Is 30:12-14) 'For the love of money is the root of all kinds of evil. And some people, craving money, have wandered from the faith, and have broken their hearts with many sorrows.' (1 Tim 6:10) We're all cracked! (crack-pots?!) Fear not, gentle reader, because, without the cracks, the Spirit could never get through to our inner souls. Any worthwhile life must be lived amidst the tensions of our weakness and brokenness. One writer speaks of the 'religious' image of us holding a golden thread in one hand, with a beautiful white swan at the end of it; while not being prepared to accept the fact that we have a big chain in the other hand, with a ferocious big black dog at the end of it! Like the moon, we tend to show just one side – the bright side – to those we meet. We all, however, have a shadow side, and we are being very dishonest and unrealistic to deny that fact. *Make Friends with your Shadow* is the title of a popular book from some years back. Within the one person there is a prodigal son, and a self-righteous brother. Our Christian calling is to become the forgiving father who brings reconciliation between the two. If I deny my brokenness, or indeed, decry it, I am not living in the truth. While this is true within the heart of the individual, it is also true within the Christian community. Such a group is like a mirror, which I take off a wall, drop on the ground, and shatter it. I then entrust one part of the broken mirror to each member of the community, and it is the unique work of the Spirit to put those pieces back together again, so that, as a community, we can reflect the face of God.

To do

The Indian guru explained to his class that there is constant war within all of us between a good animal and a bad one. When one of his pupils asked him which animal was most likely to win the battle, he was told 'The one you feed the most.' Can you identify with this in any way? Are you aware of the tussle that goes on between what you *want* to do, and what you *ought* to do; between what you *want*, and what you *need*; between what you *are*, and what you feel *called to be*? Give some thought to this today, and ask yourself if you are cracked enough for the Spirit to get through!

To say

Psalm 147

How good it is to sing to our God, how sweet and befitting
to praise him.
The Lord rebuilds Jerusalem; he gathers the exiles of Israel.
He heals their broken hearts, and binds up their wounds.

The Lord is great and mighty in power; his wisdom is beyond measure.
The Lord lifts up the humble, but casts the wicked to the ground.
He is not concerned with the strength of a horse;
Nor is he pleased with men's bravery.
The Lord delights in those who fear him,
And who put their trust in his constant love.

FIRST TUESDAY OF LENT

Human

'Then Hezekiah encouraged them with this address: "Be strong and courageous! Don't be afraid of the king of Assyria, or his mighty army, for there is a power far greater on our side. He may have a great army, but they are just human. We have the Lord our God to help us, and to fight our battles for us".' (2 Cron 32:7-8) 'Man's life on earth is a military service, his days are those of a mercenary. Like a slave, he longs for the shade of evening, like a hireling he waits for his wages. Thus I am allotted months of futility, and nights of grief and misery. In bed, I say, "When shall the day break?" On rising, I think, "When shall evening come?"' (Job 7:1-4) 'Human plans, no matter how wise or well advised, cannot stand against the Lord.' (Prov 21:30) 'Human pride will be ended, and human arrogance destroyed. Yahweh alone will be exalted on that day. The arrogance of man will be humbled; the pride of mankind will be brought low.' (Is 2:11-12, 17) We are human, a word that comes from the Latin word *humus*, meaning clay. 'Remember, man, that thou art dust, and onto dust thou shalt return.' Clay, of itself, can do absolutely nothing. Without warmth and moisture, nothing could live in clay (worms?), or grow in clay (seeds?). Of ourselves, we are totally subject to the law of gravity, and are completely incapable of raising ourselves out of the quick-sands of our own selfishness. Because I am human, I am mortal, and everything I do by my own endeavours will also die. Of myself, I can do good, but the good will not last; when I die, it will also die. I am like a tape recorder with batteries. It will play, but it will not continue to play unless it is plugged into a source of power that, of itself, it does not have.

I have sometimes imagined myself faced with the following decision: I am offered an opportunity to have a very special awareness of God's eternal love, or an opportunity to have a very special awareness of my own weakness and limitations, as a human being. I would probably opt for God's love, but I must admit that the other option is very tempting. I imagine that, if I really grasped the reality of my human limitations, that my openness to God, to his love, and to his power, would be so much more definite and consistent.

To do

A very young baby or a very elderly person are obviously quite limited in their human capacity. This, however, is not what I have in mind when I speak of human weakness. I am a prisoner in a body, and the body sets clear and definite limits to what I can do, understand, or try to achieve. I stand on the seashore, and I look out at the horizon. I know there are many more miles of water out there, but I just cannot see them. I look at the water itself, and all I can see is the top of the water. People are speaking in the distance, but I cannot hear what they are saying. And all of this is simply about the limitations of the body. Add to that all the human weaknesses we inherit because of original sin, and it's amazing that we can function at all! The point I am making is, that if God's spirit (our inner life) was taken away, the body would fall to the ground, lifeless. We own nothing. Everything we have is on loan. One heart attack, and it's all over. Without wishing to be morbid, it would be time well spent if I gave some serious thought to the reality of my humanity, to its frailties, its fragility, its mortality. *Life is fragile; handle with prayer.*

To say

Psalm 118

In anguish I cried to the Lord; he answered by setting me free.
With the Lord beside me, I need not fear. What can people do to me?
The Lord is with me, ready to help.
I can look in triumph upon my enemies.
It is better to take refuge in the Lord than to trust in the help of man.
It is better to take refuge in the Lord than to trust in the help of princes.

FIRST WEDNESDAY OF LENT

Demons

'Towards evening they brought to Jesus many possessed by evil spirits, and, with a word, he drove out the spirits.' (Mt 8:16) 'If it is by Beelzebul that I drive out demons, by whom do your own people drive them out? But if it is by the Spirit of God that I drive out demons, then the kingdom of God has already come upon you.' (Mt 12:27-28) 'Then Jesus called the Twelve disciples, and gave them power and authority to drive out all evil spirits, and to heal diseases.' (Lk 9:1) 'The seventy disciples returned full of joy. They said "Lord, even the demons obeyed us when we called on your name." Then Jesus replied, "I saw Satan fall like lightening from heaven. You see, I have given you authority over all the power of the evil one; nothing shall harm you".' (Lk 10:17-19) There is a great emphasis nowadays on working on the 'inner self', with seminars, workshops, and literature aplenty. One way of looking upon this is as an effort 'to name, claim, and tame my demons'. When I go down into the heart, I can encounter many spirits that are not of God. Ask the alcoholic, or the drug addict about their battles with the demons. We often hear reference to 'the demon drink', while drug addicts speak of having a monkey on their backs, i.e., something that clings to them, which they are powerless to shake off. We use sacramentals, such as holy water, scapulars, miraculous medals, etc., as a protection against the evil one. When I speak of demons here I am not speaking of being possessed. Rather I am speaking of a sufficient presence to be an influence on my words and actions. St Paul speaks at great length (Rom 7) about the battle going on within his spirit between doing the good or committing the evil. He concludes that there was a part of him that was in bondage, and he saw no way out of that, until he came to realise that 'Jesus has set me free.' (Rom 7:25) In the gospel we read about a man who was dumb, and who also had a demon in him. Similarly, another man who was deaf, and had a demon. Another man had so many demons in him that all attempts to chain or restrain him failed, and he spread terror throughout the region. Once Jesus walked into those situations, everything changed.

To do

Call it a demon, a weakness, a problem, an addiction, or a disposition. It matters not what you call it. Can you identify something within you that you honestly know you would be a much better person to be free of it. When it comes to addictions or compulsions of any kind, it's simple enough to put a name on my demon. Resentments, unforgiveness, jealousies, or laziness may not be that easy to spot. One Dublin woman told me of her trouble in this area, 'My mother should have called me Cleopatra, because I was the queen of *denial!*' Remember what I said above about the importance of being able to name, claim, and tame our demons.

To say

Psalm 27

The Lord is my light and my salvation – whom shall I fear?

The Lord is my battlement, my defender, I will not be afraid.
When the wicked rush at me to devour my flesh, it is they who will stumble and fall.
Though an army encamp against me, my heart will not fail;
Though war breaks out against me, I will still be confident.
One thing I ask of the Lord, one thing I seek –
That I may dwell in his house all the days of my life,
To gaze on his beauty, and seek counsel in his sanctuary.

FIRST THURSDAY OF LENT

Lost

'He deprives leaders of their judgement, leaving them to be lost in a trackless waste. Without light, they grope in the dark, and stagger like drunkards.' (Job 12:24-25) 'The Lord is close to the broken-hearted, and he saves those who are lost.' (Ps 34:19) 'Jesus sent these twelve on a mission with the instruction: "Do not visit pagan territory, and do not enter a Samaritan town. Go instead to the lost sheep of the house of Israel".' (Mt 10:5-6) 'The Son of Man has come to seek and to save the lost.' (Lk 19:10) I remember many years ago when a prominent priest left his ministry at a time when such a thing was unheard of, or certainly kept very secret. He wrote a book about his experiences, his struggles, and his thinking, which he called *Lost Shepherd in the Mist.* I read it with great interest (with the naïveté of youth), because I had often heard references to lost sheep, but never to a lost shepherd. I have discovered since just how easy it is to lose one's way in life. Jesus calls himself the Way, and he tells us that if we follow him we will not walk in darkness, but will have the light of life. I can get lost in a relationship. Relationships, by definition, are dynamic, always moving; if not forward, then certainly backwards. Quite often people find that they have drifted into a situation where a relationship seems to have just vanished, and there is nothing there any more. They never set out to do this, no more than an alcoholic ever set out to become an alcoholic. We can drift off course in anything. The few pence from the till can become embezzling on a large scale. The real problem arises when we cannot see any way back. This could account for the rise in suicides among the young in recent years. The imaginary is real to the one who imagines it, and the way back looks so dark that they choose not to face it. Yes, indeed, it is very easy to get lost. When I think of losing one's soul, I am not thinking of ending up in hell. I am thinking of adoring at the shrine of a false god, like money, power, or pleasure. Such people are truly lost.

To do

Recall some of the ideals, hopes, and expectations you had in earlier life. Some of these you have achieved, and some you have not. Are the ones who have not achieved still realistic enough to consider giving them another go? Maybe you just lost the vision, or you lost the motivation to keep going. Is there any one in particular that you should return to? Hopefully, this time you'll get it right, and you will have regained something you thought you had lost forever.

To say

Psalm 40

With resolve I waited for the Lord; he listened and heard me beg.
Out of the horrid pit he drew me, out of the quagmire in the bog.
He settled my feet upon a rock, and made my steps steady.
He put a new song in my mouth, a song of praise to our God.
Many will see and be awed, and put their trust in the Lord.
Blessed is the man who relies on the Lord, and does not look to the proud,
Nor go astray after false gods.

FIRST FRIDAY OF LENT

Exile

'I will remove the battle chariots from Israel, and the warhorses from Jerusalem, and I will destroy all the weapons used in battle. I will set your people free – free from the waterless pit of exile. Return you exiles who now have hope.' (Zech 9:11-12) 'Turn away from that evil I warned you about, the shame that weighs upon you. On that day I will face your oppressors; I will save the wounded ones, and bring back all those who are in exile.' (Zeph 3:18-19) 'Then Israel will know from that day onwards that I am Yahweh, their God. And the nations will know that Israel was exiled because they were unfaithful to me, and this is why I hid my face from them … Now, moved by my compassion for Israel, I am going to bring back those in exile, and I will give glory to my holy name. They will know that I am Yahweh their God when, after their exile among the nations, I bring them together in their own land, and leave no one behind.' (Ezek 39:22-28) Although we live in this world, we are really exiles awaiting our call to return to our True Home. I have come across some elderly people in nursing homes who experience a sort of divine home-sickness. Most of their friends and acquaintances have gone on ahead, and they are waiting patiently to catch up with them. The Jewish people have spent most of their history in one kind of exile or another, and the trouble in the Middle East is that themselves and the Palestinians are claiming the same land as their homeland. Irish families are very familiar with members who had to go into voluntary exile in order to obtain work. The absent one was the one most thought about, and most spoken about. A letter from America was shared with the neighbourhood. I have known people who have spent fifty years in America, reared a family there, and have grandchildren there, and yet they speak fondly about 'coming home' for a holiday. It would seem as if the house they lived in for the past fifty years did not qualify to be called 'home'. Home is where the heart is.

To do

Supposing you were to spread out your life in front of you like a large sheet of paper. All the details are pencilled in here and there. Is there anything here that is in exile? What I mean by that, is there any family member with whom I have an estrangement? Is there any part of my own history, my own story, that I don't want to think about, that I prefer to pretend never happened? You are as sick as your secrets. Is there anything there that I have never shared with another human being in any way, yet it weighs like a leaden weight in the pit of my stomach. Do I find anything there that I ought to *redeem, reclaim, reunite?*

To say

Psalm 42

As a deer longs for flowing streams, so my soul longs for you, O God.
My soul thirsts for God, the living God.
When shall I go and see the face of God?
Day and night my tears have been my food,
Men say to me day after day 'Where is your God?'
Now as I pour out my soul, I remember all this –
How I used to lead the faithful in procession to the house of God.
Hope in God for I will praise him again, my saviour and my God.

FIRST SATURDAY OF LENT

Longing

'I toss all night, and long for the dawn. In bed I say "When shall the day break?" On rising, I think "When shall evening come?"'(Job 7:4) 'My heart aches with longing for your ordinances at all times. Explain to me all your ordinances, and I will meditate on all your wondrous deeds.' (Ps 119:20, 27) 'Walking in the way of your laws, O Yahweh, we hope in you; your name and your memory are all the desire of our hearts. My soul longs for you in the night; for you my spirit keeps vigil.' (Is 26:8-9) 'All the world is eagerly longing for the transformation of the children of God.' (Rom 8:19) A longing is a yearning, or a vehement wish for something. We are all familiar with some of the longings of the human heart. There is some sort of hunger in there that can never be satisfied with material or earthly things, of whatever nature. St Augustine expressed it this way: 'You have made us for yourself, O Lord, and our hearts can never be at rest until they rest in you.' Nothing less than God can satisfy the longings of the human heart. The scrap-heaps of life are strewn with the human wreckage of people who chased that elusive satisfaction in all the wrong places.

I see a very special significance in Jesus sending us the Holy Spirit. The Holy Spirit would *fill* us, accompany us, teach us, guide our feet into the ways of peace, and keep us constantly in touch with the truth. The Holy Spirit, with the gifts of the Spirit, freely supplies every possible longing of the human heart; while even increasing that longing to fulfil us even more. God knows us through and through, and it is God alone who knows what our real longings are, and how those longing can be fulfilled.

To do

When I speak about longings, I am not thinking of our various human appetites for food, drink, sex, power, or money. There is always 'something else', and it can be difficult to name it, or clearly identify it. We all have dreams, and many of those dreams are achievable, if we are prepared to pay the price to make the dream come true. I have met people with a real longing to return home, no matter how many years they have spent in another country. I know people who are longing to make amends, and be reconciled with their family. I know many people who are longing for the day when they can have that last drink, or smoke that last and final cigarette. Might I suggest something for your consideration: I don't believe that God would put such a longing in your heart without providing the grace to see it through. There is nothing more powerful than an idea whose time has come. Maybe, this is *your* day?

To say

Psalm 63

O God, you are my God, it is you I seek; for you my body longs, and my soul thirsts
As a dry and weary land without water.
Thus have I gazed upon you in your sanctuary, to see your power and your glory.
Your love is better than life, my lips will glorify you.
I will bless you as long as I live, lift up my hands and call upon your name.
As with the richest food, my soul will feast; my mouth will praise you with joyful lips.

SECOND SUNDAY OF LENT

Calling

'Yahweh saw that Moses was drawing near to look, and God called to him from the middle of the bush, "Moses! Moses!" He replied "Here I am." Yahweh said to him "Do not come near; take off your sandals, because the place where you are standing is holy ground".' (Ex 3:4-5) 'On that day the Lord God Sabaoth called you to weep and mourn, to shave your head and put on sackcloth.' (Is 22:12) 'But now, O Israel, the Lord who created you says: "Do not be afraid, for I have ransomed you. I have called you by name; you are mine".' (Is 43:1) 'I have not come to call respectable people, but sinners.' (Mk 2:17) 'The gatekeeper opens the gate for him, and the sheep hear his voice, and come to him. He calls his own sheep by name and leads them out. He walks ahead of them and they follow him, because they recognise his voice. They won't follow a stranger; they will run from him, because they don't recognise his voice.' (Jn 10:3-5) 'And he called us, not only from among the Jews, but from among the pagans, too, as he said through the prophet Hosea "I will call my people those who were not my people, and beloved the one who was not beloved".' (Rom 9:24-25) *I heard the Lord call my name. Listen, too, you'll hear the same* are the words of a hymn.

Jesus identifies himself very much with a shepherd, and this was a very powerful image in the eyes and minds of his listeners. Several flocks of sheep, with their shepherds, would gather into the one large cave for the night hours. In the morning, one of the shepherds would stand outside the cave and call his sheep, and they, and only they, would come out and follow him in single file wherever he led them. Many of our mystics and saints felt called by God to take on a particular apostolate. Every founder/ foundress of a Religious Congregation heard that call. Members of my own Congregation, myself included, felt some call which brought us to where we are. Some even heard a second call, such as Blessed Damien the Leper, and they went to undertake a very different apostolate from the norm.

To do

I believe we are all called by God. Our call may not be as specific as that issued to the boy Samuel (1 Sam 3:2-14). I know people who feel called to prayers of praise, to contemplation, to caring for the homeless, to visiting the sick. They definitely seem to be aware of a special call, because they are generous in their response. An important thing to remember is: With the call comes the grace to answer the call. In other words, if I am called, I have no need to worry about how I will answer that call. Sometimes this fear prevents any answer in the first place. I said that we are all called by God and I am saying this as meaning something specific, that is over and beyond our normal everyday Christian vocation. Listen for that call today, and see if you can identify it. You will hear it, if you want to.

To say

Psalm 147

He determined the number of stars, he calls each of them
by name.

The Lord is great and mighty in power; his wisdom is beyond measure.
The Lord lifts up the humble, but casts the wicked to the ground.
With clouds he covers the sky, he waters the earth with rain,
And makes grass grow upon the hill.
He provides food for the cattle, and the young ravens when they call.

SECOND MONDAY OF LENT

Hunger

'You sent them bread from heaven to satisfy their hunger.' (Neh 9:15) 'The righteous always have enough to eat, while the wicked are always hungry.' (Prov 13:25) 'The time is surely coming', says the Sovereign Lord, 'when I will send a famine on the land – not a famine of bread or water, but of hearing the word of the Lord.' (Amos 8:11) 'He has filled the hungry with good things, and the rich he sent empty away.' (Lk 1:53) 'He who comes to me will never be hungry.' (Jn 6:35) A very popular book on prayer some years ago was called *Prayer is a Hunger.* Prayer is food for the soul, just as much as ordinary food is for the body. There is a hunger in the human spirit that food can never satisfy. Again and again we come across people who have tried to fill that hole in the heart with alcohol, drugs, sex, money, or power. At the end of the day, there is still a hunger inside, and quite often, because of lifestyle, some of these people implode, come apart, and end up very broken. The greatest hunger of all is the need to belong, the need to be loved. If prayer is a hunger, then those who pray are well nourished and healthy. This shows in action and attitude. Please note that I speak of those who pray, not those who say prayers, which is a very different thing; something that could never nourish the soul. Jesus speaks about those who 'hunger and thirst for righteousness', and he assures them they will receive that for which they yearn. Jesus also points to that particular kind of hunger to which I refer, when he tells us that those who come to him will never hunger.

Obviously, this must be a spiritual hunger to which he refers. There is something within the human spirit, and nothing less than God can satisfy it, or fulfil its hunger. Mother (Blessed) Teresa says that we, in the west, have no idea what real physical hunger is like. A small child taught her this one time. She gave the child a piece of bread to eat. The child began eating the bread, one crumb at a time. When Mother said to her 'Eat it,' the child looked at her, and said 'Mother, I'm afraid to; because when I'm finished, I'm going to be hungry again.' Once again, I refer to the promise of Jesus that they who come to him will never be hungry again.

To do

The fact that you are reading this book gives some indication that you want to nourish and nurture your soul. I have always discovered that when I became aware of my spirit being like a desert, it was because I had neglected it, by missing out on spiritual reading. I'm not thinking or speaking of big books here. There are oodles and acres of religious magazines available, and most of them do contain some very good material for nourishing the soul. I pick up a Catholic newspaper, and I am sure to get a few good articles by well-known writers, and I can gain a lot from them. Apart from this book which you now hold in your hands, might I suggest that you consider *today* what you could/should do to provide your spirit with more wholesome nourishment, through spiritual reading, of whatever kind you choose?

To say

Psalm 107

Give thanks to the Lord for he is good, for his love endures forever.

Some strayed in the wilderness and were lost, far away from the city.

They wandered around hungry and thirsty, their lives ebbing away.

Then they cried to the Lord in anguish, and he rescued them from their distress.

Let them thank the Lord for his love and wondrous deeds for men.

He quenches the thirst of the soul, and satisfies the hunger of the heart.

SECOND TUESDAY OF LENT

Emptiness

'These teachings are not empty words. It is no slight matter; on this depends your life.' (Deut 32:37) 'Eliphaz the Temanite spoke: "Should a wise man answer with empty words? Should he argue in empty words, in words that are meaningless? Your iniquity instructs your mouth, and you talk like the crafty. You are condemned by your own mouth, by your own lips, not mine".' (Job 15:1-6) 'They speak like this while taking an empty oath for a useless treaty; their sentence is growing like weeds in a ploughed field.' (Amos 10:4) 'So they have no excuse, for they knew God, and did not glorify him as befits him, nor did they give thanks to him. On the contrary, they lost themselves in their nonsense, and their empty minds are filled with darkness.' (Rom 1:21) Mary speaks of the Lord filling the hungry with good things. Jesus speaks about giving us life in abundance, of his peace, and of a joy, pressed down, and flowing over. The angel greeted Mary as being 'full of grace'. What a beautiful image; to be filled with the goodness of God. It is certainly God's wish to fill all of us with his Spirit, and to displace anything within us that is not of him. He is a jealous God, in the best sense of that word, in that his love wants to totally envelop us, and protect us from all evil.

We say that empty pots make most noise. The contemplative heart is one of quiet, and yet of much action. The work of the Spirit within is like human gestation: as time goes on, we become more and more aware of our inner life, and less conscious of any sense of emptiness.

There is an awakening going on within, and we become more and more aware of the reality, presence, and work of the Spirit.

To do

How conscious are you of your breathing? Having encountered a few heart problems over the years, I became more and more aware of just how important it is to be able to take a breath – I mean, a real deep-down breath. Drawing attention to our breathing, and entering into that process is quite often used nowadays as an approach to prayer. I can sit in silence, breathing in the Spirit (Breath) of God, and breathing out the toxins, and everything else within that is not of God. Perhaps you might spend a few minutes from time to time today doing just that. Keep this one image in your mind: Mary was filled with God's goodness, and God would love to do that in any one of us.

To say

Psalm 18

I love you, Lord, my strength.

The Lord is my rock, my fortress, my deliverer and my God, the rock in whom I take refuge.

He is my shield, the horn of my salvation, my stronghold.

I call on the Lord who is worthy of praise; he saves me from my enemies.

I called upon the Lord in my distress, I cried to my God for help,

And from his temple he heard my voice, my cry of grief reached his ears.

SECOND WEDNESDAY OF LENT

Desert

'Then the Spirit led Jesus into the desert. There he was tempted by the devil. After spending forty days and nights without food, Jesus was hungry.' (Mt 4:1-2) 'A king reigns with justice, and princes reign with righteousness. Each is like a shield from the wind, and a shelter from the rain, like streams flowing in a desert.' (Is 32:1-2) 'The wilderness and the arid land will rejoice; the desert will be glad and blossom. Covered with flowers, it will sing and shout for joy ... For water will break out in the wilderness, and streams will gush forth from the desert. The thirsty ground will become a pool, the arid land springs of water.' (Is 35:1-2, 6-7) Beneath the driest desert there is plenty of water, but it is only in very rare and special places that this water can reach the surface. Where it does, it provides an oasis, a wonderful source of life to travellers, animals, and plants alike. There are people like that; thank God for them. They are real life-givers, and life-enhancers. The human soul is like a deep deep well, with a gurgling stream of living water at the base. The problem is that the well is often cluttered up with the garbage and wreckage of life, and the water cannot possibly get near the surface. It is interesting that the Greek word for conversion is *kinosis*, which literally means to empty out. If I don't dump all the wreckage overboard, I can never become an oasis. Steps Four and Five in the AA 12-Step programme are exactly about that. Before there can be any hope of recovery, it is essential to get rid of surplus baggage. It is interesting to note that Anthony de Mello's last book, before his death, was

Unencumbered by Baggage. Edward Farrell, another very popular writer of the same era, called his last book *The Freedom to be Nothing.*

There is something very stark about a desert, and it has always been a place that drew the mystics, and the ascetics. It is significant that Jesus began his public mission by spending forty days in the desert. It is in the desert that we encounter our demons, and Jesus was no exception.

To do

If I accept that this world is a desert of sorts, and recent world events, wars, earthquakes, etc., have kept the image of desert very much to the forefront on our newspapers and television screens, then I can decide that I am willing to be an oasis. This is not something that I can actually do; rather is it something I can allow happen to me. Mary Our Mother didn't actually do anything; instead she gave God full freedom to do in, with, and through her whatever was his will. If I want to be an oasis, then I have to be willing to dump all that wreckage in the well overboard. 'Lord, give me the serenity to accept the things I cannot change.' I cannot change yesterday, because it no longer exists. In the Fifth Step of the 12 Steps it says 'We shared with God, with ourselves, and with another human being, the exact nature of our wrongs.' Note that it doesn't say that we necessarily shared what exactly we did wrong; but the nature of that wrong-doing e.g., selfishness, greed, jealousy, etc. I am as sick as my secrets. If there's anything unspoken within my spirit that needs to be shared with another, then I will never find peace until I throw that out, and get rid of it. Am I pressing any buttons in what I'm talking about?

To say

Psalm 78

They did not keep God's covenant, and refused to live by his law.

They forgot the marvels he had done, what their fathers had seen in the land of Egypt.

He divided the sea, and led them across; he made the water stand like a wall.

By day he led them like a cloud, and by night with a fiery light.

In the desert, he split rocks to give them abundant drink.

He made streams come out of a rock, and caused water to flow like a river.

SECOND THURSDAY OF LENT

Recycling?

'We know that the whole creation groans and suffers the pangs of birth. Not creation alone, but even ourselves, although the Spirit was given to us as a foretaste of what we are to receive, we groan in our innermost being, eagerly awaiting the day when God will adopt us, and take to himself our bodies as well.' (Rom 8:22-23) 'But by God's grace you are in Christ Jesus, who has become our wisdom from God, and who makes us just, and holy, and free.' (1Cor 1:30) 'This is the new song they sang: "You are worthy to take the book and open its seals, for you were slain, and by your blood you purchased for God people of every nation; and made them a kingdom and priests for our God, and they shall reign over the land".' (Rev 5:9-10) I'm not too convinced that *recycling* is the correct title for this reflection, but I have decided to go with it. What brought that word to my mind is the image of clothes in a washing machine, going though all the various cycles, and a feeling of *déjà vu* about this season of Lent. I feel I have been here before on other occasions, even if, in fact, I do not accept that. As long as I live, I will always be in need of yet another spin in the washing-machine of the Lord (right down to the 'final rinse'!).

As we become more environmentally friendly, and responsible, we are making more and greater use of the process of recycling for many materials, from paper to metal, to glass. It is to be presumed that the paper will end up as paper again, and the glass will reappear as glass once again. The recycling I had in mind when I chose the title for this reflection, is something much greater than that. It is a process of extracting the toxins, and putting more and more of God's love and mercy into the mix. We are in the process of becoming more and more into the image of Jesus Christ, even if we fall somewhat short of that ideal. The Spirit is constantly at work within our spirits, and we are in a continual process of change. I am thinking of the sculptor transforming a huge hunk of marble into an image of beauty that he had conceived in his mind. Before he begins, he already has a vision of the finished work, and he continues the process until his goal is achieved.

To do

The contemplative heart is constantly aware of this work of the Spirit. The kernel of their prayer is a constant *Yes* to what the Spirit is doing. They are like clay in the hands of the potter. Wholeness/holiness is something that happens to us, rather than anything we ourselves do. A young baby will get hair and teeth, but not as a result of anything the baby does. Spirituality is about surrender, while religion can often be about control. Just think about this image for a moment or two (it may not be as stupid as it may appear!): You are sitting in some quiet place, and you concentrate on the idea of the washing machine tumbling away within your spirit. There are many cycles, and there's a detergent, a stain remover, and a softener in the hot water. You are aware that praying is now what the Spirit is doing within you, and you give your full approval to the process. Try it today sometime, and see if it means anything to you.

To say

Psalm 49

Why should I fear when evil days come, when wicked deceivers ring me around –
Men trusting in their wealth, and boasting of their great riches?
For no one can redeem himself, or pay God the ransom for his life.
For redeeming one's life demands too high a price, and no ransom will ever suffice
For him to remain forever alive, and never see the grave.
But God will rescue me from the grave by receiving me onto himself.

SECOND FRIDAY OF LENT

New

'When Saul turned to leave Samuel, God gave Saul a new nature ... Then the Spirit of God seized him and he began to prophesy.' (1 Sam 10:9) 'But now we have been given a brief moment of grace, for the Lord God has allowed a few of us to survive as a remnant; he has freed us from slavery, and given us a new life. He has given us security in his holy place.' (Ezra 9:8) 'The stump represents a new beginning for God's people ... and just as the new branches sprout from a stump, so a new king will arise in the House of David.' (Is 6:13; 11:1) 'But forget all that – it is nothing compared to what I am going to do. For I am about to do a brand-new thing. See, I have already begun! Do you not see it? I will make a pathway through the wilderness for my people to come home.' (Is 43:18-19) 'The Lord says "I am making a new earth, and new heavens".' (Is 65:17) 'I will give you a new heart, and a new mind.' (Ezek 36:26) Because God is the Creator, he can also recreate. 'My God is new with every new day.' (Cardinal Suenens). Each new day has its own unique possibilities, as has each new baby that is born. God is not into sticking-plaster and cellotape. It is essential to keep this in mind when I stand before God. The only limits to what he does in our lives are the ones we set. Everything that God does is new. No two individuals have the same finger-prints, or the same DNA. Each person is completely unique, because God does not repeat himself.

When I think of my own resolutions, promises, and

good intentions, I cannot fail to notice just how repetitious they are; how I've been here so many times before. At the time of writing, I have stopped smoking again! How long does it take us to accept the simple fact that, of ourselves, we cannot create, or recreate! On our own, it is 'just more of the same'. On New Year's Day, or Ash Wednesday, I find myself making the very resolutions I made one year ago! Nothing new about that! There seems to be some sort of stubborn resolve within many of us, convincing us that we can fix things, make all things OK, and get life back in control! The *ego* is an extraordinary bully. EGO could well stand for Edging God Out! In my head, I know this, but in my heart, I often wonder if I really believe this. There seems to be some sort of basic rebelliousness within us that will fight God all the way, determined that I can do what, in my heart, I know that only God can do.

To do

I used the word 'surrender' in the last reflection. This is a difficult concept for our human pride to accept. To surrender is to admit that I am defeated, and no one likes to admit to this. It is difficult to stop playing God, especially after years of 'religion', when we believed that we had to save our own souls, and to 'merit' heaven, as a reward for a life well spent. If I had kept a record of my resolutions over the years, I would find the same old 'cookies' cropping up again and again. When am I going to learn? It is more than just a question of rearranging the deck-chairs on the Titanic! This is serious stuff, and deserves to be taken more seriously. What is it, in your life, that you have been trying to 'fix'? Do you really want to change, to change utterly? Then you will have to stop playing

God, and surrender to a Power greater than yourself. God can do for you what you never could do for yourself. Even God cannot resolve a problem until we hand it over to him. What is it that you cling to, and refuse to get out of the way? Remember St Augustine's prayer: 'Lord, make me chaste, but not yet.'

To say

Psalm 18

I love you, O Lord, my strength.
The Lord is my rock, my fortress, my deliverer and my God, the rock in which I take refuge.
He is my shield, the horn of my salvation, my stronghold.
I call on the Lord who is worthy of praise; he saves me from my enemies.
Torrents rushed at me in a destroying flood.
Caught as by the cords of the grave, I was utterly helpless before the snares of death.
But I called upon the Lord in my distress, I cried to my God for help.
And from his temple he heard my voice, my cry of grief reached his ears.

SECOND SATURDAY OF LENT

Salvation

'Salvation comes from the Lord.' (Jonah 2:9) 'Now thou dost dismiss thy servant in peace, O Lord, because mine eyes have seen your salvation, which you have prepared before all the people.' (Lk 2:30) 'And all of mankind will see the salvation of God.' (Lk 3:6) 'Salvation is to be found through Jesus alone.' (Acts 4:12) 'And so I bear everything for the sake of the chosen people, that they, too, may obtain the salvation given to us in Christ Jesus, and share eternal glory.' (2 Tim 2:10) 'Besides you have known the scriptures from childhood; they will give you the wisdom that leads to salvation, through faith in Jesus Christ.' (2 Tim 4:15) 'Although he was the Son, he learned through suffering what obedience was, and once made perfect, he became the source of eternal salvation for those who obey him.' (Heb 5:8-9) Salvation is not something we receive when we die; it is the grace we are offered that enables us start again any day, or any moment we want to. To be saved implies that, in some way, we were lost. Usually being lost means that I may know where I am, but I don't know where to go from here. I can be lost in a relationship just as easy as in a jungle. Immediately next door to where I am writing there is a nursing home, with a very elderly age-profile. One day, a visitor came in and forgot to close the front door. It was some time later when I met Joe (not his real name), two blocks away, and he was completely oblivious of the fact that he was totally lost. He just kept walking, totally unaware or unconcerned about where he had been, or where he might end up. When I suggested that he should come for a walk with me, he turned around meekly, and came back down the road with me. There is a difference between being lost and going astray. If I go astray, there's a chance that I'll find my way back. If I'm lost, I'm lost, and I'll ask or pray for help!

To do

When you find yourself going around in circles, always ending up at the same place, chances are you're lost! We can experience this in many ways in life. We experience it with resolutions, decisions, and good intentions. There is nothing more powerful than an idea whose time has come. So much time is wasted, because *now* is not the time to act – but 'some other time'. All diets begin on Monday. On the outskirts of Dublin, a new housing project was being built. A large hoarding by the side of the road was sure to get the attention of the passer-by: 'If you lived here, you would be home now.' I think of this sometimes when I find myself making a resolution about something that I made on many another occasion. 'If I had stayed off the fags back then, I wouldn't have to stop again today. If I hadn't taken that first drink, I would still be a Pioneer today.' I said already that salvation is the grace I get to start again today. I'm sure you can think of something that needs your attention; something that has been on the back-burner for far too long. If you are waiting until it becomes easy to do, then it may never get done. *Do it … do it … today!*

To say

Psalm 71

In you, O Lord, I seek refuge; let me not be disgraced.
In your justice deliver me, turn your ear to me and save me.
Be my rock of refuge, a stronghold to give me safety,
For you are my rock and my fortress.
You, O Lord, have been my hope, my trust, O God, from my youth.
O God, be not far from me; my God make haste to help me.
I shall always hope and praise you more and more.

THIRD SUNDAY OF LENT

Invitation

'Messengers were sent out with invitations from the hands of the king and his officials for every part of Israel and Judah. They had orders from the king to say: "People of Israel, come back to Yahweh, the God of Abraham, of Isaac, of Israel, and he will come back to those of you who are left, and have escaped the grasp of the kings of Assyria".' (2 Chron 30:6) 'I invited you so often, but you didn't come. I reached out to you, but you paid no attention.' (Prov 1:24) 'The kingdom of heaven can be illustrated by the story of a king who prepared a great wedding feast for his son. Many guests were invited, and when the banquet was ready, he sent his servants to notify everyone that it was time to come. But they refused … Then the king said to his servants, "The wedding feast is ready, and the guests I invited aren't worthy of the honour. Now go out to the street corners and invite everyone you see".' (Mt 22:2-3, 8-9) Most invitations have RSVP written on them, asking those receiving them to confirm if they will be there or not. Not to reply at all is still a reply! The main difference between good and evil is that good invites, while evil compels. One is a host, the other is a bully. God invites us, while Satan attacks us. God doesn't give me anything; he offers me everything. The onus is on me whether I choose to accept his offer or not. Jesus didn't want Judas to go out and hang himself, but he wouldn't stop him. He didn't go around healing anybody, no more than he does today. He goes around with the power to heal, and it is up to the person along the way to decide whether they want what he offers, or they decide to let him pass by. 'Jesus of Nazareth is passing by,' Bartimaeus was told. Bartimaeus was faced with a choice. He could remain silent, and settle for dying as a blind man, or he could grab the moment of grace, call out, and have his sight restored. Thankfully, he did the latter. We all have such moments in our lives. We all are presented with those moments of grace, when the onus is entirely on us. There is absolutely no ambivalence or hesitation on God's side. God has irrevocably and eternally committed himself to our good and welfare. The rest is up to us. 'In this is our salvation: his blood, and our faith.' (Rom 3:22) Jesus has completed his side of the Covenant, and it is entirely up to us whether we avail of that or not. As I implied earlier, 'no' is also an answer.

To do

'The road to hell is paved with good intentions.' Someone else said yes for you at your baptism, and you may not been too seriously involved in any commitment at confirmation. We are invited to become fully-fledged members of the family of God. When a baby is adopted, the natural mother usually has about six months, before actually signing the papers, and confirming the adoption. During that six months, she is free to change her mind. We all were issued with certificates of baptism and confirmation, but they may not be too prominent on our bedroom walls. What I'm talking about here is that, with or without a certificate, I should renew my own personal acceptance of the invitation issued to me by God. He is a personal God, and he awaits a personal commitment. I can do this in any way I choose, and it can be extremely simple, while being totally sincere.

To say

Psalm 4

Answer me when I call, O God, my justice!
When I was in distress, you gave me solace.
Have compassion on me and hear my plea.
O sons of men, how long will you harden your hearts?
How long will you delight in deceit?
How long will you love falsehood?
But you must know that the Lord has shown his kindness
to me.
When I call to him, he hears me.
I lie down and sleep in peace, for you alone, O Lord,
Make me feel safe and secure.

THIRD MONDAY OF LENT

Rescue Plan

'Go now! I am sending you to Pharaoh to rescue my people, and bring the children of Israel out of Egypt.' (Ex 3:8) 'As for the prophet or dreamer, he must die, because he has spoken to draw you away from Yahweh, your God, who brought you out of Egypt, and redeemed you from the house of slavery.' (Deut 13:6) 'He rescued us from the power of darkness, and transferred us to the kingdom of his beloved Son. In him we are redeemed and forgiven.' (Col 1:13) 'The Lord will rescue me from all evil, bringing me to his heavenly kingdom.' (2 Tim 4:18) I often think just how easily I could take the whole work of redemption for granted. It is not possible for me to have any understanding of the absolute necessity of a plan of salvation for me, because, of myself, I haven't the remotest chance of bettering my human condition. Only God can do a God-thing, and only the Creator can recreate. On a human level, I can change things here and there, like appearance, attire, physique, or language. There is no possibility whatever of changing the inner self, the real me. It is because of this fact that Jesus came and, if I were the only person on this planet, he would still have to come, if I were to be rescued and redeemed. Early on in the recent war in Iraq, the Americans got great mileage out of the fact that their troops had raided an Iraqi hospital, and rescued a young women soldier. As it happened, she was quite severely wounded and, even if afforded a chance, she could not have escaped on her own. Imagine the reaction of her rescuers, who risked their lives in the process, if she refused to allow them remove her from the hospital. I don't think it would have taken much persuasion!

'By your cross and resurrection, you have set us free.' We are not free, of course, until we begin to exercise our freedom. Jesus is not going to drag us anywhere against our will. We cannot enjoy 'the freedom of the children of God' unless we choose to. How free we are, or will ever become, depends totally on ourselves.

To do

It's rather scary to think that, of ourselves, we can completely reject, or miss out on God's rescue plan for us. If there is any reason, more than others, for this *To do* section in these reflections, it is because I feel a great need to stress again and again just how responsible we are for what God can do in, with, and through us. It can be so easy for us to drift along, happy-go-lucky, without a serious thought in the world, and fail to grasp how vital it is that each of us take personal responsibility for our Christian vocation. Let me be specific. Supposing I am caught in bondage to substance abuse, to gambling, to pilfering, or to lust. Does this rescue plan of God apply here? Of course it does! When I am ready to stop playing God, to fall on my knees and ask for help, then God will be free to step in and take over. Can you identify an area in your life where you need a miracle, because all your efforts to date have failed? OK, go for it *today*.

To say

Psalm 106

Give thanks to the Lord, for he is good, for his love endures forever.
Who can count the Lord's mighty deeds, or declare all his praises?
Blessed are they who always do what is just.
Remember me, O Lord, when you show favour to your people.
Rescue me when you deliver them, let me see the triumph of your faithful;
Let me share the joy of your nation, and join your people in praising you.
He delivered them many a time, but they went on defying him, and sinking deeper into their sin.
But he heard their cry of affliction, and looked on them with compassion.
Remembering his covenant, he relented for their sake, because of his great love.

THIRD TUESDAY OF LENT

Gospels

'I have complete confidence in the gospel; it is God's power saving those who believe, first the Jews, and then the Greeks. The gospel shows us how God makes people upright through faith.' (Rom 1:16-17) 'Then he told them "Go out to the whole world, and proclaim the gospel to all creation. They who believe, and are baptised, will be saved; they who refuse to believe will be condemned".' (Mk 16:15-16) 'Peter spoke up and said "We have given up everything to follow you." Jesus answered, "Truly, whoever has left house or brothers or sisters, or father or mother, or children, or lands, for my sake, and for the gospel, will not lose his reward. I say to you he will receive a hundred times as many ... And in the world to come he will receive eternal life".' (Mk 10:28-30) The word 'gospel' means 'good news'. From the very beginning, this was promised to 'all the people'. It wasn't the case that all the people were willing and ready to listen to the good news. If Jesus waited for that moment to come, he wouldn't have started yet! There is nothing automatic about the gospels. The fact that I may be familiar with them means nothing, if I don't believe them, and act on them.

Being familiar with the gospels could mean nothing more than giving them some sort of mental assent up in the head; and that is certainly not faith! The faith required to accept the gospels should be in the heart, and in the feet. I show that I believe the gospels when I show that I live them. *You write a new page of the gospels each day, by the things that you do, and the words that you say. People read what you write, whether faithful or true. What is the gospel according to you?* The gospels provide a blue-print for life and living, as they point out a very clear Way, which is Jesus. The gospels is our rescue map in the jungle of life. It is very clearly marked, has sure and certain directions, and gives fixed and firm guarantees on delivering all of its promises.

To do

I wrote a book last year based on the promises in the gospels. It was quite a revelation to discover that there are 156 promises in all, and each is quite definite, and presented in simple language. Not once did I find the words maybe, perhaps, or might. Jesus said 'The sin of this world is unbelief in me.' Elizabeth said to Mary 'All these things happened to you because you believed that the promises of the Lord would be fulfilled.' As I was working my way through the promises, I realised that I had been making a serious mistake for many years. Time and again, year in, year out, I was making promises to God. Of course, quite often today's promise was one I made once a month for several years past. Not a very good track record, I must admit! By the time I had finished the book, I had reached a simple and obvious conclusion: I stopped making promises, and I tried to take his promises seriously. Just imagine how your life would change if you selected a few of those promises, prayed about them, reflected on them, and began to claim them. Jesus said that heaven and earth would pass away before one of his promises would pass away. I said that there are 156 promises in all, but I'll just pick three for your attention at this time. *The Father will surely give the Spirit to those who ask. If you love me, you will obey me, and then you can ask the Father for anything in my name. If you forgive, you are forgiven.*

To say

Psalm 1

Blessed is the man who never follows the counsel of the wicked,
Nor stands in the way of sinners,
Nor sits where the scoffers sit;
Instead he finds delight in the law of the Lord,
And meditates day and night on his commandments.
He is like a tree beside a brook, producing its fruit in due season,
Its leaves never withering.

THIRD WEDNESDAY OF LENT

Me

I would have to take undue liberties with the bible to find references to *me!* Any such word is when God speaks about himself. I chose this title rather spontaneously, and I believe I had some positive reason for doing so. Many of us tend to be very good when it comes to sweeping generalities, e.g., proper minimum wage, equal opportunities, food for the hungry, etc. The test of our sincerity and commitment, however, is when we are ready to mediate that down to the specific. When it comes to me paying a wage, how does my action measure against my generality? I may be all in favour of housing travellers or asylum-seekers, but not in my backyard, thank you. I think my reason for choosing *me* as a title for this reflection is that I wanted to make sure that I just wasn't tiptoeing around issues, and keeping well out of reach of myself. I must gratefully admit that I myself get enormous blessings in the course of my writing, because I write for me; I reflect on each item, at it applies to me; and I measure my own performance against the standards I am setting out for others. I do not pretend that I can change much in my life through changing my thinking, or how I see things. I believe it works the other way around. If I am prepared to change my actions, that, in turn, will begin to change my thinking. It took me a long time to pick up that simple bit of wisdom. Although I intend running with it now, I do have some misgivings about the *To do* part of each day's reflection. I would like to be more specific, but have decided against that, in trusting the goodness and goodwill of the readers to do that themselves. I hope and trust that my confidence in, and respect for the reader is well-placed, and that something definite and concrete will surface, that is in need to attention *today*.

To do

I said that I write for me, and the thought of someone else reading my thoughts is an added bonus and blessing. Might I suggest, gentle reader, that you ensure that you're reading this for *you!* No place for speed-reading here, or, like the cow filling one stomach with grass, and then bringing it all back up again at a later time to be chewed, and put in stomach number two! One of the ways that helps is if you take it that this reflection is a letter you received in the post this morning. You sit down, take time out, and you read it. If you have to reply to the letter, you will take greater care about all the points it contains. Sometimes when I have to reply to a letter, I use a highlighter pen on the important points to be covered in my reply. If it is an e-mail, I print it off, and do the same, before replying. I'm still not convinced that my choice of *Me* was a good one (!), but I hope that it draws both writer and reader deeper into the plot! St Paul was afraid that, having preached to others, he himself might become a castaway.

To say

Psalm 139

O Lord, you know me; you have scrutinised me.
You know when I sit and when I rise; from far away you discern my thoughts.
You observe my activities and times of rest; you are familiar with all my ways.

Before a word is formed in my mouth, you know it entirely, O Lord.
From front to back you hedge me round, shielding me with your protecting hand.
Such marvels are beyond me, too lofty for me to attain.
It was you who formed my inmost part, and knit me together in my mother's womb.
I thank you for the wonders you have done, and my heart praises you for your marvellous deeds.

THIRD THURSDAY OF LENT

Garden

'God planted a garden in Eden in the east, and there he placed man, whom he had created. Yahweh God made grow out of the ground every kind of tree that is pleasing to see, and good to eat, also the tree of Life in the middle of the garden, and the tree of the Knowledge of Good and Evil.' (Gen 2:8-9) 'Then Yahweh God said "This man has now become like one of us, making himself judge of good and evil. Let him not stretch out his hand to take and eat from the tree of Life as well, and live forever." So God cast him from the garden of Eden to till the soil from which he had been made.' (Gen 3:22-23) 'This is what Yahweh says "You were the model of perfection, full of wisdom, and perfect in beauty. You lived in Eden, the garden of God, and every kind of precious stone adorned you. I anointed you a guardian angel on the holy mountain of God, where you walked amidst the spirits of God. You were perfect in your ways, from the moment you were created, until wickedness was found in you".' (Ezek 28:13-14) I finished a book within the past year called *Look At It This Way*. It dealt with the story of redemption as one where Jesus ran after us, and invited us to come back to the Garden, and all would be forgiven. The story of the Prodigal Son encapsulates the core of the gospel message. *Come back to the Garden. There's a big hug waiting for you, even if you have got pig's food all over your face.*

As we travel these days of Lent together, we will join Jesus in another garden, where the battle becomes intense, and he is facing up to 'the final enemy' which is death. Adam and Eve said *No*, and Jesus would say *Yes*, and this would cost him his life. 'Greater love than this no one has, that someone would lay down a life for a friend.' I am much more tolerant and compassionate towards the apostles as I continue my own journey, and I have the benefit of hindsight, something denied to them. There was no way that they could possibly grasp the full significance of what they witnessed. All of that would become clearer after Pentecost, because it is only the Spirit who can lead us into the secrets and plans of God. As we continue on our *Road To Resurrection*, we can also think of it as our journey back to the Garden.

To do

The catechism I used in my early school days told me that 'God created us to know, love, and serve him, and by this means, to gain everlasting life.' That latter part presented me with many problems throughout my life, until I realised that it was not true! There is no way that I can gain everlasting life! When we speak of forgiveness, redemption, salvation, or heaven, we are speaking of pure free gift. If it were possible for us to *gain* eternal life, then Jesus need not have come in the first place. Romans 3:22 tells us that our salvation depends on two things only: Christ's blood and our faith. In other words, Jesus gained salvation for us, enabling us to return to the Garden, if we are prepared to accept that gift, and act on it. Jesus asks us to follow him, because he *is The Way*. There is no other way to get back to the Garden. If we follow him, we will not walk in darkness, but will have the light of life. Jesus asks for a decision, not a discussion. These days of Lent are slipping by, and it is time that we faced up to some serious decisions. Once again, I remind myself and yourself that the grace to do anything in this area is pure gift, or else we're back to making promises again!

To say

Psalm 9

Let my heart praise the Lord. I proclaim all your marvellous deeds.
I rejoice and exult in you. I sing praise to your name, O Most High.
The Lord is a rampart for the oppressed, a refuge in times of distress.
Those who cherish your name, O Lord, can rely on you,
For you have never forsaken those who look to you.
For he who avenges blood remembers,
And has not turned a deaf ear to the cries of the multitude that suffer.

THIRD FRIDAY OF LENT

Weeds

'Evil men sprout like weeds in the sun, entwining their roots around a pile of rocks, holding fast to each stone. But if uprooted, the place rejects it as its own, and there it lies rotting by the road, while other plants grow in its place.' (Job 8:16-17) 'I walked by the field of a lazy man, the vineyard of one lacking sense. I saw that it was overgrown with thorns. It was covered with weeds, and its walls were broken down.' (Prov 24:30) 'My people have sown wheat, but are harvesting weeds. They have worked hard, but it has done them no good. They will harvest a crop of shame, for the fierce anger of the Lord is upon them.' (Jer 1213) 'The kingdom of heaven can be compared to a man who sowed good seed in his field. While everyone was asleep his enemy came and sowed weeds among the wheat, and left.' (Mt 13:24-25) Everything that God creates is good. In the Creation narrative, we are told that God looked at each new creation, and 'He saw that it was good.' When God created us he saw that we were good, and he still sees that goodness in us. Like the good wheat, an enemy has sown weeds among the wheat. The word Satan means enemy. The weeds that Satan sowed were not of God's creation – sin, sickness, and death. The farm labourers asked the farmer if he wanted them to pull up the weeds, and he told them not to, because they would only damage the wheat in the process. He said that, at the right time, he himself would take care of the weeds. It was to remove those three weeds that Jesus came. Through his life, death, and resurrection, Jesus would remove the weeds of sin, sickness, and death. Over the next few days, I will deal with each of these in separate reflections. The point I want to stress here is that only God can restore his creation to its original purity. Those of us who have been around for a while have vivid memories of all the methods used in religious exercises, whereby we ourselves were expected to do the weeding. Steps Six and Seven of the Twelve Step programme, used in recovery from addictions, read as follows: *We're entirely ready to have God remove these defects of character. Humbly asked him to remove our shortcomings.* This can never be a do-it-yourself job. Notice the words *we're entirely ready*. In other words, we had to stop playing God, and not attempt something that only God can do.

To do

It is so easy for us to allow the ego to take over, and to think that we can be all-conquering, no matter how often our failures have shown us otherwise. This pride and deep-rooted rebelliousness is a direct result of Original Sin. Adam and Eve wanted to be as powerful as God, and that sin is no longer very original, as we can fall into this trap every day. In a way, I can see how or why this can happen. As a human being, I can do good. The danger here, of course, is, because I myself am mortal, any good I do of myself is also mortal, and will not last. Most alcoholics can stop drinking for a day or two, but their sobriety will be short-lived, unless they are ready to fall on their knees and surrender to a Power greater than themselves. A tape-recorder with batteries will play, but it cannot continue to play. If, however, it is plugged into a power that it does not have in itself, it will continue to play. How many cul-de-sacs have you found yourself in during the course of your life? Do you think you might be ready to surrender, and hand a situation over to the care of an all-powerful God, who can do for us what we never can do for ourselves?

To say

Psalm 57

Have mercy on me, O God, have mercy, for my soul takes refuge in you.
I will find shelter in the shadow of your wings till the disaster has passed.
I call on God the Most High, on God who has done everything for me.
Send from heaven a Saviour, and put my oppressors to shame.
May God send me his kindness and love.
Be exalted, O God, above the heavens! Your glory be over all the earth.
My heart is steadfast, O God, my heart is steadfast. I will sing and make music.
I will give thanks to you, O Lord, among the peoples; I will sing praise to you among the nations.
For your love reaches to the heavens, and your faithfulness to the clouds.

THIRD SATURDAY OF LENT

Sin

'Forgive the sins of your people and bring them back to the land you gave to them and to their ancestors.' (2 Chron 6:25) 'I confess that we, the people of Israel, have sinned. My ancestors and I have sinned.' (Neh 1:6) 'A man shall not die because of his father's sins; no, he will live. His father, instead, who practised extortion and stole from others, will die for his sin, because he did wrong among his people ... The person who sins is the one who will die. If the sinner turns from his sin, observes my decrees, and practises what is right and just, he will live, he will not die.' (Ezek 18:19-24) 'God is the only one who can forgive sins.' (Lk 5:21) I draw your attention to the fact that I have chosen sin as the theme for today's reflection, and again for tomorrow's. This is a deliberate decision. I want to begin (today) by looking at sin as something that happened to me; as something that was committed against me, where I am the victim of sin. Because of Original Sin, my human nature is irretrievably and irrevocably damaged, with a hole in the ozone layer of my spirit that only God can recreate, and make all things new again. It is important to remember that I am damaged property, and do not have within myself the resources to better my human condition. St Paul was a truly wonderful apostle and man of God, and yet he could say this about himself: 'I don't understand myself at all, for I really want to do what is right, but I don't do it. Instead I do the very thing I hate. I know perfectly well that what I am doing is wrong, and my bad conscience shows me that I agree that the law is good. But I can't help myself, because it is sin inside me that makes me do these evil things. I know I am rotten through and through as far as my old sinful nature is concerned. No matter which way I turn, I can't make myself do right. I want to, but I can't. When I want to do good, I don't. And when I try not to do wrong, I do it anyway.' (Rom 7:15-20) Enough of Paul, who goes on with more of the same. Let us dip in again at the end of what appears to be total and utter despair. 'Oh, what a miserable person I am! Who will free me from this life that is dominated by sin? Thank God, the answer is in Jesus Christ Our Lord; he has set me free.' (Rom 7:24-25)

To do

In tomorrow's reflection, we will look at some of the sins we commit; but it would be a mistake to approach that scenario without being deeply aware of the damage done to my nature through sin I myself did not commit. In my more day-dreaming moments, I have reflected on the following possibility (which I have already used in a previous reflection): I am given a choice – to have a privileged insight into the extent of God's love for me, and the extent and depth of my own human weakness. I would probably be drawn to God's love, but I would dearly love to have the other insight as well! I honestly believe that it would make a profound difference in my life if I became fully aware of just how weak and powerless I am. I imagine that it would cause me to throw myself with complete abandon into the arms of a loving God, in whom alone is my hope. 'Unless you see signs and wonders, you will not believe', says Jesus. (Jn 4:48) I do not ask for signs and wonders, and will continue to trust the Spirit to reveal my own weaknesses to me. It is not necessary to get tied up in addictions and compulsions to become aware of just how weak I really am. It is uniquely the work of the Spirit to lead me into all truth, and my own basic weakness is one of those fundamental truths. Once again, I refer to Paul's assessment of his human condition, and his profound awareness of just how weak he was. To come to realise, accept, and understand this weakness is fundamental in my openness to the grace of salvation and redemption that is offered us in Jesus Christ.

To say

Psalm 3

O Lord, how great in number are my foes!
How numerous are they who rise up against me!
How many are they who say to my soul:
There is no help for him in God.
But you are my shield , O Lord, my glory; you lift up my head.
Aloud I cry to the Lord, and from his holy hill he answers me.
If I lie down to sleep, again I awake, for the Lord supports me;
No fear of the thousands standing around me.
Arise, O Lord! Deliver me, O my God!
Salvation comes from the Lord, may your blessing be upon your people.

FOURTH SUNDAY OF LENT

Sin

'People don't care if they sin, but good people will always dwell among the upright.' (Prov 14:9) 'And they shall call him Jesus, because he will save his people from their sins.' (Mt 1:21) 'The Son of Man has authority on earth to forgive sins.' (Mt 9:6) 'They confessed their sins, and he baptised them in the river Jordan. (Mk 1:5) 'Forgive us our sins, as we forgive all those who have sinned against us.' (Lk 11:4) 'In the meantime, the tax collector, standing far off, would not even lift his eyes to heaven, but beat his breast, saying "O God, be merciful to me, a sinner".' (Lk 18:13) There we have it, right there! That's the secret of salvation. The publican has arrived at a place where he has no doubt whatever about admitting that he is a sinner. This is an extraordinary moment of grace. Most of my generation were put in the Holy of Holies (with the Pharisee!), with all the rules, regulations, and religious practices that would ensure that we would never ever 'fall' into sin. That sure was a recipe for disaster. For several years, I tried desperately to cling to this position, not knowing that I didn't belong there in the first place. It is a long journey from the place of the Pharisee to the place of the Publican but, hopefully, life will bring us on that journey. Holiness, whatever we conceive of it to be, means that I come to a conviction that I'm a bigger sinner than I ever thought I was. I stand in front of a strong spotlight. As I approach the light, I become more and more aware of the specks of dust on my sweater or jacket. The nearer I come to God, the more obvious my sins become. There was a time in my earlier life when I entered a confession box to declare that I had no sins to confess, while, just to justify my presence, I mentioned a few things 'from my past life'. I can smile at that now, without condemning it, because that's where I was at that time. I find some hope in the fact that I have no scarcity of material when I stand before the Lord, with the canvas of my life opened out fully before him. Sin is not so much an action, as an attitude. One kind act doesn't mean that I am a kind person; I could be a candidate in the next general elections! Sin is pride, unbridled *ego*, self-will run riot. It involves putting myself before God and others, and meeting my needs at the expense of someone else. Sin involves mediating death to myself, and to those around me. Jesus came that we should have life, and have it in abundance. Sin is putting myself over and above all other concerns, and placing myself at the centre of my existence.

To do

There is a healthy balance between being conscious of my sins, and being scrupulous, or guilty. To admit to sin is to face the truth; because if God wanted a permissive society, he would have given us ten suggestions, instead of ten commandments! When I celebrate Eucharist, it is interesting that I use the first person singular on three occasions only: I confess … I have sinned … Lord, I am not worthy. All the remainder of the Mass is plural, but, when it comes to sin, I must speak for myself only, and leave the others alone. I begin the Mass by calling to mind my sins; at the consecration I say 'shed for you and for many for the forgiveness of sin'; and at communion time, I say 'This is the Lamb of God who takes away the sins of the world.' We are speaking of sin here, not holiness, and it is significant that Jesus was condemned because 'He welcomed sinners, and even ate with them.' (Mk 2:6) I mentioned earlier in this reflection that it can be a very long journey from the Holy of Holies down to the back of the Temple, where the publican is. There are times in my life when I am aware of some movement in that direction. Are you more convinced now that you are a sinner than you were some years ago? It is not a question of committing more sins, but being more aware of my weakness and powerlessness. 'There, but for the grace of God', is a very sobering slogan. As life goes on, I should be less and less inclined to throw that first stone.

To say

Psalm 37

Do not worry over evil people, nor be envious of wrongdoers.
For they will fade as the green herb, and soon be gone like withered grass.
Trust in the Lord, and do good, dwell in the land, and be at peace.
Make the Lord your delight, and he will grant your heart's desire.
Commit your ways to the Lord; put your trust in him, and let him act.
Then will your vindication come, beautiful as the dawn,
And the justification of your cause, bright as the noonday sun.

FOURTH MONDAY OF LENT

Sickness

'Yahweh will remove from you all sickness, and he will not let any of the plagues of Egypt, which you have known, fall upon you.' (Deut 7:15) 'If they suffer from any plague or sickness, whatever be the prayer or supplication of anyone showing repentance, and raising his hands in the direction of this house, then listen from heaven, your dwelling place, and forgive.' (1 Kgs 8:37) 'Outside in the open is the sword; plague and starvation in the houses. Those in the country will die by the sword; those in the city will be victims of famine and sickness. Those who escape will go to the mountains, they will be like doves, each one moaning because of his sin.' (Ezek 7:15-16) 'Jesus went all over Galilee, teaching in their synagogues, proclaiming the good news of the kingdom, and curing all kinds of sickness and diseases among the people.' (Mt 4:23) 'And these are the signs that will accompany those who believe in me … They will place their hands on the sick, and they will get well.' (Mk 16:18) There is a difference between sickness and suffering. St James makes a very clear distinction between the two. 'Are any among you suffering? They should keep on praying about it. And those who have reason to be thankful should continually sing praises to the Lord. Are any among you sick? They should call for the elders of the church, and have them pray over them, anointing them with oil in the name of the Lord. And their prayer, if offered in faith, will heal the sick, and the Lord will make them well. And anyone who has committed sins will be forgiven.' (Jas

5:13-15) This is a simple test to distinguish between sickness and suffering. Sickness is not from God. Let me explain. Enough nicotine, alcohol, or other destructive substances, then don't blame God if you get sick. 'By their fruits you will know them.' (Mt 12:33) Sickness is suicidal, in that it is self-inflicted. Please be patient with me as I explain this further. I am in a hospital ward. There are two patients in opposite beds, each with an identical chart at the foot of the bed. One is sick, the other is suffering (which is a special vocation). The person who is suffering will be concerned how I am feeling, and will tell me about someone in the unit who is seriously ill. It will take some time for me to remember that he/she is the person in hospital, because their concern is for others. Whatever is wrong with that person is clearly from God, because the results are very edifying. When I go to the other bed, and ask how the patient is, I will get a tirade about the staff, the tea is too hot, the porridge is too cold; and if I were there for an hour, I would never be asked how I am. Whatever is wrong with this person is clearly not from God, because I cannot discover any good coming from it.

To do

I went on a bit in that reflection, so I will keep this section quite short. Suffering is a very special vocation that is given to few. Such people are chosen souls. The body is *not* me. I am living in the body for an infinitesimal part of my existence. Only the body grows old; the person inside is still a child. The body could be rotten with cancer, while the person inside could be very healthy indeed. I myself spent some time, on occasions, in ICU units, with my body wired up to several machines. I was very conscious, and grateful that, within my heart, I was very much at peace, and didn't think of myself as being sick. This was a good experience, and it taught me a great deal. What has your experience being during those times when the body was finding it increasingly more difficult to keep all the vital organs going? Do you have any memory of how *you* yourself were doing?

To say

Psalm 6

O Lord, in your anger, do not reprove, nor in your fury punish me.
Have mercy on me, O Lord, for I have no strength left.
O Lord, heal me, for I have no strength left.
O Lord, heal me, for my bones are in torment.
My soul also is greatly troubled. How long, O Lord, how long will you be?
Come back to me, O Lord, save my life, rescue me for the sake of your love.
The Lord has heard my plea; the Lord will grant all that I pray for.

FOURTH TUESDAY OF LENT

Death

'When our perishable being puts on imperishable life, when our mortal beings put on immortality, the word of scripture will be fulfilled: Death has been swallowed up by victory. Death, where is your victory? Death, where is your sting?' (1 Cor 15:54-55) 'We know that we have left death, and come over into life, because we love our brothers and sisters. He who does not love remains in death. He who hates his brother is a murderer, and you know that eternal life does not remain in the murderer.' (Jn 3:14-15) 'I have authority over death, and the world of the dead.' (Rev 1:18) 'Sin entered the world through one man, and his sin brought death with it and, as a result, death has spread to the whole human race.' (Rom 5:12) Death is the final enemy, the last of the three weeds sown among the good wheat. It was essential that Jesus is clearly seen to have overcome death, because 'if Jesus did not rise from the dead, our faith is in vain.' (1 Cor 15:14) *Dying, you destroyed our death; rising, you restored our life. By your cross and resurrection you have set us free; you are the Saviour of the world.* When Jesus went down into the Jordan river to be baptised, we are told that 'the heavens were opened', the Father's voice was heard, and the Spirit was seen to physically come upon him. When he bowed his head in death, we are told that 'the veil of the Temple was rent in two'; in other words, for the first time ever, the Holy of Holies was accessible to all of God's people. I can share in the death of Jesus in a very personal way. When I was baptised, water was poured upon my head.

Every time I come to Mass, I bring that water back, one drop at a time, and I place it in the chalice, uniting my little dyings of everyday living with the death of Jesus. For the Christian, death is like a pile of sand at the end of my life, which I can take and sprinkle, a few grains at a time in my everyday living. When was the last time you died for anybody? 'Greater love than this no one has.' I am called on to die to my selfishness, my opinions, my pride, and my ego for the sake of those around me. Dying is something I can do every day of my life. If I wait till the end of my life to die, it could be too late.

To do

'Everybody wants to go to heaven, but nobody wants to die.' Self-preservation is the strongest human instinct. I honestly believe that if I can situate death as being a central part of life, then I have some hope of taking it on board as a fact of life. When a baby is born, the only thing we can be certain of is that, one day, this baby will die. The baby is born to die. I particularly like the Christian teaching on death, because it deals with one of the central issues of life. Jesus laid great stress on the truth of his resurrection, and his victory over death. He spent forty days with his disciples after his resurrection, because they were to be witnesses to his resurrection. His triumph over death represented his greatest and most significant victory in restoring us to eternal life. Because of what he accomplished, he completely undid all the evil of Original Sin, and he made it possible for us to return to the fullness of life in the Garden. I ask you, please, to give some serious thought today to the whole question of death for the Christian. If you get this one, you are well on your way to the fullness of life here, and hereafter.

To say

Psalm 27

The Lord is my light and my salvation – whom shall I fear?
The Lord is my battlement, my defender; I will not be afraid.
When the wicked rush at me to devour my flesh, it is they who stumble and fall.
Though an army encamp against me, my heart will not fail;
Though war break out against me, I will still be confident.
One thing I ask of the Lord, one thing I seek –
That I may dwell in the house of the Lord all the days of my life,
To gaze on his beauty, and seek counsel in his sanctuary.
I hope to see the goodness of the Lord in the land of the living.
Trust in the Lord, be strong and courageous; – yes, put your hope in the Lord.

FOURTH WEDNESDAY OF LENT

Saviour

'They abandoned God their Creator, and rejected their mighty saviour.' (Deut 32:15) 'God is indeed my saviour; in him I trust and am not afraid, for the Lord is my strength. He is my song: He has become my saviour.' (Is 12:2) 'My soul proclaims the greatness of the Lord, my spirit exults in God my saviour.' (Lk 1:46-47) 'God did not send the Son into the world to condemn the world; instead, through him, the world is to be saved.' (Jn 3:17) 'After that many more believed because of his own words, and they said to the woman "We no longer believe because of what you told us; for we have heard for ourselves, and we know that this is the Saviour of the world".' (Jn 4:41-42) 'It is from the descendants of David that God has raised up the promised saviour of Israel, Jesus … Brothers, children, and descendants of Abraham, and you also who fear God, we have been sent to give you this message of salvation.' (Acts 13:23, 27) When Jesus walked the roads of Galilee, he was Saviour; one who brought salvation, forgiveness, and healing to those who asked him. He was not Lord yet, because he had not triumphed on Calvary, or Easter morning, nor could he give the Spirit. He was Saviour who, when he returned in triumph to the Father, was made Lord, given full authority over everything in heaven and on earth, and all the enemies of God were put under his feet. Throughout the history of the Jewish people, they offered sacrifices for the forgiveness of sins. This could be anything from a lamb to an ox. When Jesus came, he was recognised by John the Baptist as the Lamb of God, who takes away the sins of the world. His sacrifice need never be repeated, because it was a new and eternal sacrifice, that bridged the gap for all time between God and his people.

To do

There is no point in speaking about a Saviour to someone who is not convinced of the need for salvation; to speak of a Saviour to someone who is not convinced of being a sinner, needing a Saviour. Jesus told us that the Spirit would 'convict us of sin', because, as a Spirit of truth, he would lead us into all truth. It is interesting to note that Jesus had great success with the sinners, marginalised, and the outcasts. This must surely have been because they were open to him, having few choices in the whole area of making friends, and being accepted. It is almost as if, by some instinct, that this is shown. When he was in the house of one of the Pharisees, a woman, who was a public sinner, entered the house. It is reasonable to assume that her appearance caused some consternation among the Pharisee's friends who were gathered there. With an extraordinary level of trust and confidence, the woman went straight to Jesus, and fell at his feet. For whatever reason, she seemed assured that he, of all those in that house, would not reject her. And her courage and trust were rewarded, and Jesus spoke very powerfully in her defence. Do you believe that you could show the same understanding and compassion to yourself, as Jesus displayed in his treatment of this woman? Guilt is not from God. 'Satan is the accuser of our brothers; he accuses them day and night before God.' (Rev 12:10)

To say

Psalm 40

With resolve, I waited for the Lord; he listened and heard me beg.
Out of the horrid pit he drew me, out of the quagmire in the bog.
He settled my feet upon a rock, and made my steps steady.
He put a new song in my mouth, a song of praise to our God.
Many will see, and be awed, and put their trust in the Lord.
Blessed is the man who relies upon the Lord, or does not look to the proud, nor go after false gods.
Do not withhold from me, O Lord, your mercy; let your love and faithfulness preserve me constantly.

FOURTH THURSDAY OF LENT

Healing

'I am the Lord, the one who heals you.' (Ex 15:26) 'Let their hearts be hardened, make them deaf and blind, lest they hear and see, and their hearts understand. Yet if they came back to me, I would have healed them.' (Is 6:10) 'Jesus went all over Galilee, teaching in their synagogues, proclaiming the good news of the kingdom, and healing all kinds of sickness and diseases among the people.' (Mt 4:23) 'But now, Lord, see their threats against us, and enable your servants to speak your word with all boldness. Stretch out your hand to heal, and to work signs and wonders through the name of Jesus your holy servant.' (Acts 4:29-30) When I stand before Jesus, I can do so for forgiveness, for healing, or to be empowered by his Spirit. At the moment of death, I will stand totally naked before God – nothing hidden, no denying, no pretending, no excusing. All that is over. Why should I wait till I die to do this, because I can do it right now? Healing is a very encompassing word. It would be a mistake to think of it as something I pray for when I have cancer, or some other life-threatening disease. We are *always* in need of healing. When I am totally healed, you will read my death notice in the papers! Jesus heals from the inside out. I couldn't imagine him healing a blind man, and letting him go down the road filled with resentment against his brother. Such a person was certainly not healed.

Jesus didn't go around healing anybody. He went around with the power to heal, and the person on the roadside had to make a decision. If Bartimaeus had not called out, stopped Jesus, and asked that he might see, he would certainly have died a blind man. (Mk 10:46) This is just as true today. Healing is a continuous process, just as it is with medical treatment. The ten lepers were sent on their way to show themselves to the priests, as evidence that they were healed. In actual fact, when they left Jesus, they still had leprosy but, taking him at his word, they went on their way, to discover that their leprosy began to disappear. Jesus laid great stress on *belief* as a requirement for healing. 'Do you believe I can do this? Your faith has healed you.' Once again, as with our salvation, this is brought about by 'his blood and our faith'. (Rom 3:25) A very good example of what I have in mind is the decision of the little woman in the crowd who thought 'If I can only touch the hem of his garment, I will be healed.' (Mt 9:21)

To do

Being a member of the church is like going to a hospital where everybody is sick, including the Matron! We are all in need of healing, and this need is so diverse that none of us can be exactly sure where the *real* need is. As I said earlier, the Lord heals from the inside out. Because of our human condition, there is a lot of healing needed within the human spirit. This is a life-long process. Recovering alcoholics are not bad people trying to become good, but sick people who are trying to become well. If you ever waken up some morning, and find that your life is exactly the way it should be, then, don't move – just wait for the undertaker! Most of what requires healing in our lives would never show up in an X-ray. There are people walking around today, and no X-ray would show anything wrong with them and, yet, in many ways, they are very sick people. I have dealt with people whose body was ravished with cancer, but the person inside, the *real person*, was very healthy indeed. What do you think might show up if you had a *spiritual* X-ray today? Just for now, I ask you not to think of the body, as you reflect on how healthy you think you are.

To say

Psalm 146

Praise the Lord, my soul! I will sing to the Lord all my life;
I will sing praise to God while I live.
Do not put your trust in princes, in mortal man who cannot save.
His spirit leaves him, he goes back to the earth.
On that very day his plans come to nothing.
Blessed is he whose help is the God of Jacob, whose hope is in the Lord his God,
Maker of heaven and earth, the sea and all they contain.
The Lord is forever faithful; he gives justice to the oppressed, and gives food to the hungry.
The Lord will reign forever, your God, O Zion, from generation to generation.

FOURTH FRIDAY OF LENT

Anointing

'You will put all these ornaments on your brother Aaron, and his sons. You will then anoint, invest, and consecrate them to serve in the priesthood.' (Ex 28:41) 'These you are to make into a holy oil for anointing, such a blend as the perfumer might make. With it you are to anoint the Tent of Meeting, and the ark of the Statement.' (Ex 30:26) 'Then Moses took the anointing oil, and anointed the Holy Tent, and everything in it, to consecrate them. He sprinkled the altar seven times, and anointed the altar and its furnishings.' (Lev 8:10-11) 'Make him leave his companions, and bring him to a place apart from them. There you shall take the bottle, and pour the oil on his head, saying: "Yahweh has anointed you king of Israel".' (2 Kgs 9:2-3) Anointing has always been an important part of religious ceremonies. We were anointed at baptism, confirmation, some of us at ordination, and, hopefully, all of us at death. Anything that is anointed with blessed oil becomes sacred, and that is why even a new-born baby is anointed under the chin, and on the crown of the head. The reason for anointing under the chin is a symbolic breast-plate, or coat of armour for protection; and anointing on the head is like being consecrated as sacred. At confirmation we are anointed on the forehead, as an outward sign of some inner commitment. During the sacrament of the sick, the person is anointed on the forehead, and on the palm of each hand. The anointing on the forehead is a sign of being a sacred person, belonging to God, while the anointing on the hands is a symbol of opening our hands and letting go; of submission to God, and to what he thinks is best for us. St James tells that 'If anyone is sick, he should call on the elders of the church, and they should pray over him, anointing him with oil, and, their prayer, if offered in faith, will heal him.' (Jas 5:14-15) Jesus himself was called the Anointed one of God, because he came with healing, forgiveness, and empowering.

To do

There are many kinds of anointing, but surely the greatest anointing of all must be an anointing by the Holy Spirit. There is no way that I could possibly exaggerate the importance of the work of the Spirit in our lives. With this anointing comes the power to open our hearts fully to all that Jesus came to give us. The Spirit came to complete Jesus' work on earth, and to bring us to the fullness of grace. Without the Spirit, we do not have what it takes to avail of, and to make full use of the redemption effected through the life, death, and resurrection of Jesus. Jesus did what he did, but nothing happens to us until we are ready and willing to avail of all that he earned for us. On Easter Sunday morning, nothing happened to anybody but Jesus. That very evening, his apostles would probably have denied him, and run away once again. They had to wait for their Easter, which we call Pentecost. On Easter morning, the stone was rolled back from the tomb; on Pentecost morning, the doors of the upper room were flung open. Only then were the apostles free; only then could they come into the fullness of their inheritance. John the Baptist said that he baptised with water, but another was coming after him would anoint with the Holy Spirit, and with fire. Pentecost is the ultimate anointing, and *we all need a Pentecost.* Have you ever prayed for a Pentecost in your life? 'The Father will surely give the Spirit to those who ask.' (Lk 11:13)

To say

Psalm 89

You are our glory and power, and your favour lifts us up.
Our king is in the hands of the Lord; the God of Israel is our shield.
In the past you spoke in a vision; you said to your faithful people:
'I have set a crown upon a mighty one; on one chosen from the people.
I have found David my servant, and with my holy oil I have anointed him.
My hand will ever be with him, and my arm will sustain him;
No enemy shall outwit him, nor wicked man oppress him.'

FOURTH SATURDAY OF LENT

Reconciling

'Sin will be forgiven, and eternal reconciliation will be established.' (Dan 9:24) 'So, if you about to offer your gift at the altar, and you remember that your brother has something against you, leave your gift there in front of the altar, go at once and make peace with your brother, and then come back and offer your gift to God.' (Mt 5:24) 'From enemies, we have become at peace with God through the death of his Son; with much more reason now we may be saved through his life. Not only that; we feel secure in God because of Christ Jesus, our Lord, through whom we have been reconciled.' (Rom 5:10-11) 'All of this is the work of God who in Christ reconciled us to himself, and who entrusted to us the ministry of reconciliation. Because in Christ God reconciled the world with himself, no longer taking into account their trespasses, and entrusting to us the message of reconciliation.' (2 Cor 5:18-19) 'Through him God willed to reconcile all things to himself and, through him, through his blood shed on the cross, God establishes peace on earth as in heaven.' (Col 1: 20) Jesus bridges the gap between God and man, between heaven and earth. Through Adam and Eve we were alienated; through Jesus we are reconciled. He has one hand in the Father's hand, and the other hand held out to us. As in the story of the Prodigal Son, he is begging us to come home, where a divine amnesty awaits us. It is not possible for our feeble human minds to fully grasp the extent of this love, but we have the Holy Spirit, who is more than ready and willing to do this for us. 'Reconcile' is defined as 'make friendly after estrangement'. It gives us some glimpse into the evil of sin when we realise that we chose to be estranged from a God who is *love.* While we might not readily admit to insanity, we must admit that our actions can often be insane. Insanity involves doing the same things again and again, and expecting different results each time. I think we can all put our hands up for this one. I am not speaking of guilt here, but a willingness to admit to behaviour that is grossly insane. However, we must remember, that the basic reconciliation is concerned with our willingness to reverse the evil of Original Sin, and return to the Father's hug in the Garden, and to begin all over again.

To do

Again and again I stress our own personal involvement in this process. No matter what Jesus has done, nothing happens in our lives until we are willing to tap into this, and to accept his salvation on a personal level. There is nothing automatic about God, or what Jesus has done for us. The X factor is our willingness to latch onto this, and to accept this as our personal gift and privilege. Nobody else can do this for me. Jesus is a *personal Saviour*, and he becomes my Saviour when I deliberately and personally accept him as my personal saviour. When I speak of reconciliation, I am also speaking of reconciliation within myself. This reconciliation involves the self-righteous brother being reconciled with the Prodigal, Martha being reconciled with Mary, Cain being reconciled with Abel. Once again, I refer to that book *Make Friends With Your Shadow.* Each one of us can have many areas that are quite alienated, and are not accepted as part of who and what we are. Holiness means wholeness, and this involves *all* of me being accepted as part of who and what I am. Instead of being 'all over the place, very scattered, badly in need of getting myself together', I begin to come together, *all of me*, and I stand before God exactly as he sees me right now. I can do this any day I choose – so, why not *today?*

To say

Psalm 73

But my heart was so embittered, my spirit so distraught,
 that I failed to understand.
I was like a stupid beast in your presence.
Yet I shall always remain with you; you hold my right hand.
You guide me with your counsel and, in the end, you will
 take me to glory.
I have no one in heaven but you; on earth, I desire nothing
 but you.
God is my portion forever.
Those who abandon you will perish; you destroy all who
 are unfaithful to you.
I have made the Lord my refuge, and I will proclaim all
 his works.

FIFTH SUNDAY OF LENT

Openness

'And the moment he came out of the water, heaven opened before him, and he saw the Spirit coming down on him like a dove. And these words were heard from heaven, "You are my Son, my beloved one, whom I have chosen".' (Mk 1:11) 'God then opened her eyes, and she saw a well of water. She went and filled the skin, and gave the boy a drink.' (Gen 21:19) 'God saved the wretched through their suffering, he opens their eyes to their misfortune.' (Job 36:15) 'In that day deaf people will hear words read from a book, and blind people will see through the darkness.' (Is 29:18) 'Then everyone who can see will be looking for God, and those who can hear will listen to his voice.' (Is 32:3) 'You will open the eyes of the blind, and free the captives from prison. You will release those who sit in dark dungeons.' (Is 42:7) As I write I realise that we are into the fifth week of Lent, and I have hardly mentioned the word 'Lent' at all! This was not deliberate; it was just me cruising along with my musings and reflections, without any road map, beyond the leading of the Spirit. As the days and weeks pass by, however, it is time to become more specific about the season that is in it, and how we are preparing for Easter; for that time when death is overcome, and we are set free. By now, we should be more in touch with a sense of expectation, and of excitement. Easter is *for real*, and this could be the greatest moment of grace in my whole life. Hopefully, some of the material in these reflections will already have opened up new horizons, or given new insights.

If I go out after a shower of rain, there is one thing I may notice. In one place is a pool of water, while close by, the ground is already quite dry. In one place, the earth is open and receptive, and the rain is instantly absorbed; while, nearby, the earth is packed so tightly that nothing can penetrate it. People are like that. Some people are so uptight, or so blinded with bigotry, that nothing can get through; while others are deeply moved by the simplest scene, gesture, or occasion. It is the work of the Spirit to enable us to open our hearts to the word of God. Clay, without moisture or warmth, is incapable of producing, or preserving life. Without God's Spirit within our hearts, nothing of God can get through.

To do

Try to become more aware of your breathing today. Most of us go about our daily tasks, usually completely unaware of this extraordinary life-giving action, that just keeps going. The first thing we do when we're born is take a breath, and it's the last thing we do as we die. When we are doing exercises, like jogging, for example, we need much deeper, and more frequent breaths, and the lungs are expanded to allow for this. This is a process of opening up that might help us remember what I have in mind in today's reflection. I breathe deeply of God's Spirit, and become aware of that Spirit entering into the very core of my being. I can whisper words like 'Spirit and Breath and Power of God.' Openness to God is simply a heightened awareness of my desire to receive him, to have him in my life, to live with his life.

To say

Psalm 24

The earth and its fullness belong to the Lord, the world and all that dwell in it.
Who will ascend the mountain of the Lord? Who will stand in his holy place?
Those with clean hands and pure heart, who desire not what is vain,
And never swear a lie.
Lift up, O gateways, your lintels, open up, you ancient doors,
That the King of glory may enter.
Who is the King of glory?
The Lord of Hosts, he is the King of glory.

FIFTH MONDAY OF LENT

Crying Out

'The sons of Israel groaned under their slavery; they cried to God for help, and from their bondage, their cry ascended to God.' (Ex 2:23) 'And when he cries to me I will hear him, for I am full of pity.' (Ex 22:26) 'So we called out to Yahweh, the God of our fathers, and Yahweh listened to us.' (Deut 26:7) 'And as they were stoning him, Stephen prayed, saying: "Lord, receive my spirit." Then he knelt down, and said in a loud voice: "Lord, do not hold this against them." And when he had said this he died.' (Acts 7:59-60) 'Then, no more fear; you did not receive a spirit of slavery, but the Spirit that makes you adopted children, and every time we cry *"Abba, Father"*, the Spirit assures our spirits that we are children of God.' (Rom 8:15-16) There are many references in scripture to God listening to the cries of the poor. The Israelites had to bear many hardships, including slavery, exile, and foreign domination. They had nowhere to turn but to Yahweh, their God. One side of the coin shows that they were a long-suffering people; while the other side shows the many ways and means that God used to answer their cries for help.

Prayer can be anything at all, as long as it's a form of loving communication with a loving God; sometimes prayer of deep contemplation, and often prayers of quiet desperation. There are times when I really need to cry out to God from my heart. It's not that he doesn't hear if I whisper, but my prayer must surely echo around heaven when it comes as a cry from the heart. I don't believe it possible for a human being to fall on his/her knees, cry out to God, and not be heard. A cry from the heart results from brokenness and pain, and must surely reach the heart of a loving God.

To do

I must confess that I don't have to think for any great length of time to come up with something in my life that requires the prayer of screaming! What I mean by this is there is something there that has certain characteristics about it that is not a run-of-the-mill problem. I could have a serious illness, a deep depression, a compulsive pattern of behaviour that is destructive to myself, and to those around me, an addiction to substance abuse of any kind, and so the list goes on. Desperate diseases require desperate remedies. There comes a time when I'm sick and tired of being sick and tired, and I decide that I've had enough. Ready to scream yet? A scream or a cry from your heart doesn't have to be heard by those around you! The prayer is a scream when it comes from the very depth of my soul, from the bowels of my being. It is a cry for help, and it is a cry that may not be heard by those around you, but most certainly will be heard by God.

To say

Psalm 28

To you, O Lord, I call; my rock, be not deaf to me.
For if you heed me not, I shall go down to the pit like the rest.
Hear my cry for mercy as I call on you for help,
As I lift up my hands toward your innermost sanctuary.
Blessed be the Lord! He has heard my cry for help.
The Lord is my strength, my shield, in him my hearts trusts.

I have been helped, and my heart exults, with my song I give you thanks.
The Lord is the strength of his people, the saving refuge of his anointed.

FIFTH TUESDAY OF LENT

Leprosy

'Yahweh said to Moses and Aaron, "If someone has a boil, an inflammation or a sore on his skin which could develop into leprosy, he must be brought to Aaron the priest, or to one of the priests, his descendants. The priest shall examine him, and if the hair on the sore has turned white, and the sore appears to be deeper than the surrounding skin, then it is indeed the sore of leprosy. When the priest sees this, he shall declare that person unclean".' (Lev 13:1-3) 'Yahweh struck down the king. He became sick with leprosy, and he remained a leper till the day of his death.' (2 Kgs 15:5) 'Then a leper came forward. He greeted him respectfully, and said "Sir, if you want to, you can make me clean." Jesus stretched out his hand, touched him, and said "I want to; be clean again." At that very moment the man was cleaned from his leprosy.' (Mt 8:2) 'Go back and tell John what you have seen and heard: the blind see, the lame walk, the lepers are made clean …' (Mt 11:4-5) Leprosy is a still very much present in today's world. One of the members of my own Congregation is Blessed Damien the Leper. There are still lepers on the island where he worked, lived, and died.

For our purposes, I speak of leprosy as anything unclean that I need to be rid of. It doesn't have the external visual evidence of leprosy, but it can still be quite debilitating and slowly destructive. The psalms sing of the 'man with clean hands and pure heart'. Jesus accused the Pharisees of their meticulous attention to all external details while, within their hearts, they could be rotten through and through. He compared them to marble sepulchres, lovely on the outside, but full of rotting bones inside. This time of Lent coincides with the beginning of 'spring cleaning' time. It is something like this that I have in mind in today's reflection. There is no progress made along the road to resurrection unless we clean house first.

To do

This 'house/heart cleaning' can cover many things. It can include clearing the wreckage of the past, learning the lessons from it, and moving on. It can include any area of sexual deviance, an area that seems to expand with each new day. The enormous exploitation of the sex industry, and the endless bombarding that invades even our private homes through television, Internet, etc., all of this makes it increasingly more difficult to have and to hold a moral ethic which, while not being prudish, does have clear and definite guidelines. If leprosy was considered unclean, then what of the porn-peddlers, and those who trade in child pornography? I honestly believe that, if I am not contaminated or polluted by that in any way (and I know quite a lot of people who are not), then I still have an obligation, through conscious and deliberate prayer, to be an advocate before God for all the innocent victims of such horrible and evil exploitation. I can 'adopt' these victims as my 'special people', and make them a very important part of my daily prayers before God.

To say

Psalm 73

Surely God is good to the virtuous, to the clean of heart.
But, as for me, I almost stumbled, I nearly lost my foothold.
For I was envious of the arrogant when I saw them prosper in their wickedness.
Their mouths defy the heavens, and their tongues dictate on earth.
People, therefore, look up to them, and lap up every word they utter.
'How will God ever find out?' they say.
'Is everything known to the Most High?'
Such are the wicked – always carefree while they rake in riches.
In vain have I kept my heart clean, and washed my hands in innocence.
But now my joy is to be near God;
I have made the Lord my refuge, and I will proclaim all his works.

FIFTH WEDNESDAY OF LENT

Blindness

'But the men inside the house stretched out their hands to bring Lot inside the house, to save him, and then they shut the door. As for those at the entrance to the house, they were struck with blindness, from the smallest to the largest, so that they were unable to find the door.' (Gen 19:10-11) 'I will guard and support you, for I have given you to my people as the personal confirmation of my covenant with them. And you will be a light to guide all nations to me. You will open the eyes of the blind, and free the captives from prison. You will release those who sit in dark dungeons.' (Is 42:6-7) 'After Jesus left the girl's home, two blind men followed along behind him, shouting "Son of David, have mercy on us." They went right into the house where he was staying, and Jesus asked them "Do you believe that I can make you see?" "Yes, Lord", they told him, "we do." Then he touched their eyes and said "Because of your faith, it will happen." And suddenly, they could see.' (Mt 9:27-30) 'Then the disciples came to Jesus and asked "Do you realise you offended the Pharisees by what you just said?" Jesus replied "Every plant not planted by my heavenly Father will be rooted up. So ignore them. They are like blind guides leading the blind, and if one blind person guides another, they will both fall into a ditch".' (Mt 15:12-15)

There are many ways in which I can be effected by blindness. The one that interests me here is blindness of the spirit, a blindness that seriously and adversely effects my living life to the full. I may not see God at work in my life. I may not see God in others, and be blinded by bigotry, racism, or intolerance. I could suffer from 'tunnel-vision', and see very little outside my own immediate concerns and interests. A person who is physically blind could have much deeper insights and visions into the wonders of life with God than a sighted person might have. I have a friend who, while sighted, also has a sharp sense of God's work in her life, and I have learned a great deal from her ability to see what is well beyond the human vision. This is a gift of the Spirit, and a very precious one indeed.

To do

That last sentence provides us with a starting point. When I open my heart to the Spirit, the eyes of my heart will be opened. It is the unique work of the Spirit to lead us into all truth and, therefore, we are brought to see the truth. This is the perfect and divine antidote for all forms of blindness that gives rise to racism, bigotry, and intolerance of all kinds. When the eyes of the body close in death, the eyes of the soul open out to the wonders of eternity, infinity, and to see the Face of God. This process can begin right now as you read this. There are many stories in the gospels about Jesus restoring sight to the blind. Imagine what could happen when Jesus enters my heart at communion time. 'Do you believe that I can make you see?' was the question he answered the two blind men who followed him into a house. I am asked that very same question. Another important question is 'Do you really want to see?' The onus is on each one of us, because Jesus tells that us that 'to give sight to the blind' is one of the reasons why he came. As I am writing this, and as you read it, I pray that the Spirit might cause the scales to fall from the eyes of our hearts, because 'blessed are the pure of heart, for they shall see God.'

To say

Psalm 146

Praise the Lord, my soul! I will sing to the Lord all my life.
I will sing praise to God as long as I live.
Do not put your trust in princes, in mortal man who cannot save.
His spirit leaves him, he goes back to the earth,
And on that day his plans come to nothing.
Blessed is he whose help is in the God of Jacob,
Whose hope is in the Lord his God,
Maker of heaven and earth, the seas and all they contain.
The Lord is forever faithful; he gives justice to the oppressed,
And gives food to the hungry.
The Lord sets prisoners free, and gives sight to the blind.

FIFTH THURSDAY OF LENT

Dumbness

'Great crowds came to Jesus, bringing the dumb, the blind, the lame, the crippled, and many with other infirmities. The people carried them to the feet of Jesus, and he healed them. All were astonished when they saw the dumb speaking, the lame walking, the crippled healed, and the blind able to see; so they glorified the God of Israel.' (Mt 15:30-31) 'The people were completely astonished, and said "He has done all things well; he makes the deaf hear, and the dumb speak".' (Mk 7:37) 'They are one people, and they have one language. If they carry this through (Tower of Babel), nothing they decide to do from now on will be impossible. Come! Let us go down, and confuse their language, so that they will no longer understand each other.' (Gen 11:6-7) 'These were dispersed, and peopled the islands of the nations, each with their own language, according to their tribes and their nations.' (Gen 10:5) 'On the morning of Pentecost … all were filled with the Holy Spirit, and began to speak other languages, as the Spirit enabled them to speak. Staying in Jerusalem were religious Jews from every nation under heaven. When they heard this sound, a crowd gathered, all excited because each heard them speaking in his own language.' (Acts 2:4-6)

Speech is a wonderful gift but, like any of God's gifts, it can be abused and misused. Actually having vocal cords, and the words, could still mean that I could be quite dumb. Not speaking my truth when I should, or using my speech to destroy or harm another, is a form of dumbness much worse than not being able to make a sound in the first place. The spoken word, like feathers in the wind, cannot be taken back. We all know of wonderful prophets of our own day who refuse to remain silent, and what they said cost them their lives. They could have remained silent, just as Jesus could have remained silent when he stood before the religious leaders, but this would be the worst possible form of dumbness, because it involves moral cowardice, and denial of the truth. If I think of speech as a very special and precious gift, then I will treasure that gift, and I will realise just how destructive it can be when I allow a devil of dumbness to keep me silent, when the gift of speech was needed.

To do

The tongue can be a two-edged sword; it can build up, or pull down; heal or hurt; create or destroy. One of the surest proofs that the Spirit of God lives within a person is the facility that person has to confirm others, and make them feel worthwhile. There is a direct connection between Pentecost and confirmation, as distinct from the sacrament of that name. 'Send me the flowers now, be they pink, or blue, or red. I'd rather have one blossom now than a truckload when I'm dead'! I sometimes joke that if you want to hear nice things about a person, you should go to his funeral! Please send me the flowers when I can still smell them! I don't think God would be very impressed when we tell him we're sorry, we thank him, or we praise him, if the people in my life don't hear that first.

To say

A passage from James' letter, chapter 3, as a prayerful reflection:

'A person who commits no offence in speech is perfect, and capable of ruling the whole self. We put a bit in a horse's mouth to master it and, with this, we control the whole body. The same is true of ships: however big they are, and driven by strong winds, the helmsman steers them with a tiny rudder. In the same way, the tongue is a tiny part of the body, but is capable of great things … We use it to bless God our Father, and also to curse those made in God's likeness. From the same mouth come both blessing and curse.' *(I strongly recommend that you, gentle reader, might read all of this chapter of James' letter.)*

FIFTH FRIDAY OF LENT

Deafness

'What Israel was looking for, it did not find, but those whom God elected found it. The others hardened their hearts, as scripture says, "God made them dull of heart and mind; to this day, their eyes cannot see, nor their ears hear".' (Rom 11:7-8) 'If today you hear his voice, harden not your hearts, do not be stubborn, as at Meribah, in the desert on the day of Massah, when your fathers challenged me, even though they had heard my words, and seen my deeds.' (Ps 95:8-9) 'They have ears but they hear not.' (Mt 13-13) 'They heard the message, but it did them no good.' (Heb 4:2) 'Scripture says "If you hear God's voice, do not be stubborn as they were in the place called Rebellion." Who are those who, having heard, still rebelled? They were all those who came out of Egypt with Moses.' (Heb 3:15-16)

There are none so deaf as those who don't want to hear. Listening is a very important part of prayer. If I am willing to listen, God is always willing to speak. His Spirit is continually communicating with us, and when we pray from the heart the Spirit of God is in the words we use. While I pray, it is important to remember that God has a few things to say to me also, so I should give him a chance to get a few words in sideways! Prayer is not always me talking to God who doesn't hear; but it's often God speaking to me, who won't listen. Pilate asked Jesus 'What is truth?', and then he walked away before Jesus answered his question. (Jn 18:38) In today's world, it's becoming more and more difficult to find moments or places of quiet. There's a radio on all the time in most kitchens, and in most cars. Being part of a generation who grew up on 'giving up something for Lent', it might not be very acceptable to suggest that the radio and television sets should be given longer breaks during Lent, and times for quiet reflection be encouraged. I met a couple recently, who, to me, were a seven-day wonder. They have four of a family, whose ages range from 23 down to 11, and they have never had a television set in the house! What impressed me most is that the family was really alive and fun-loving, and very much into making their own music, and engaging in their own pastimes.

To do

No, I'm not going to suggest 'giving up' anything. It might prove more fruitful and productive if I gave some serious thought to the whole idea of listening to God. Supposing I stood at a church door as people were leaving after Mass, I wonder how many of them could give me some idea about what the readings of the Mass were, and what are the points they remember from those readings. (I might 'skip' any questions about the homily!) Seriously, though, I am thinking of Jesus speaking about those who have ears but do not hear. He said 'I will not judge the world; the words I have spoken to them will judge them. If I had not come and spoken to them, they would have an excuse for their sin.' (Jn 15:2). I am being very deliberate in not suggesting things to do, because I trust the Spirit within the heart of each reader to do a much better job at that than I could ever hope to do.

To say

Psalm 50

The God of gods, the Lord has spoken, and summoned the earth from the rising of the sun to its setting.
He calls to the heavens above, and to the earth below, that he may judge his people:
'Gather before me, my faithful ones, who made a covenant with me by sacrifice.'
The heavens proclaim his justice, for God himself has come to judge.
'Hear, O my people, listen. I will testify against you, O Israel. I am God, your God.
Give this a thought, you who forget God. Give me thanks with offerings, and honour me,
Do right as well, and I will show you the salvation of God.'

FIFTH SATURDAY OF LENT

Crippled

'But when I stumbled they gathered in glee and, to my surprise, began to strike me; even cripples who were strangers to me fabricated charges against me. These men who would mock a cripple, made me the butt of all their ridicule.' (Ps 35:16) 'He who sends messages by a fool is cutting his own feet. Like the unsteady legs of a cripple, such is a proverb in the mouth of fools.' (Prov 26:6-7) 'They were crippled and far from home, but I will make a great nation out of them.' (Mic 4:7) 'Great crowds came to him, bringing the dumb, the blind, the deaf, the lame, the crippled, and many with other infirmities.' (Mt 15:30) In a way, I suppose these reflections are intended to help us enter into the spirit of this time, and not remain as onlookers, or simply readers of events that happened all those years ago. It helps if I remember two very central points: *The gospel is now, and I am every single person in it.* I have my own blindness, my own deafness, my own demons. There are many many ways in which a person can be crippled, and being physically disabled is but one of those. Being emotionally crippled must be the severest form. Victims of serious child abuse must be very severely damaged emotionally. It must be so very difficult ever to trust again, and to be open to a loving, caring relationship. The human psyche is a very delicate commodity indeed, and can be easily traumatised, and severely damaged.

As we approach Calvary (Good Friday), and go on to Easter, this might be a good time to become aware of any areas in which I may be crippled. Because of hurts in the past, I may find it difficult to trust, to love, to forgive. I will pick up on this in the next section.

To do

I don't like the word 'crippled', but will continue to use it in its broadest sense. Drug addicts and alcoholics are badly crippled. People suffering from depression are severely crippled in their ability to enjoy life. Many people are severely crippled in childhood through violence in the home, or other unhealthy situations there. This can leave scars for life, and many never really fully recover from that. Because of being 'put down', passed over, getting raw deals, etc., many people have to live with a very poor self-image, and lack of confidence. I would suggest that, while those early years might explain how I feel today, I cannot allow that to continue as an excuse for how I am. I did not have control over those years, but I can surely get help today to overcome them, and to leave them behind. 'Lord, give me the serenity to accept the things I cannot change.' I cannot change the past, but it has a great deal to teach me. The only value the past has are the lessons it taught me. Any compassion I may have has come out of my own experience of brokenness and hurt in my own life. It would be a pity to waste all that experience, when others can benefit from my compassion and understanding. The programme of Alcoholics Anonymous works on the principle that only one alcoholic can fully and properly understand another. I can turn a problem into an opportunity, and others can benefit enormously from my own experience of pain and suffering. God never wastes a thing. He can turn all things into good. That will be the core of our reflection for Good Friday.

To say

Psalm 4

Answer when I call, O God, my justice!
When I was in distress, you gave me solace.
Have compassion on me, and hear my plea.
Be angry, but do not sin.
Search your heart when you are in bed, and be still.
Many ask 'Who will show us what is good?'
Let your favour shine on us, O Lord!
I lie down and sleep in peace,
For you alone, O Lord, make me feel safe and secure.

PALM SUNDAY

Donkey

'Fools, for I also had mine hour, one far fierce hour and sweet. There were shouts about mine ears, and palms before my feet.' (Chesterton) 'Issachar is like a sturdy donkey. He bends his back to the burden, and submits to forced labour.' (Gen 49:14) 'If you see your enemy's donkey going astray, take it back to him. When you see the donkey of a man who hates you falling under its load, do not pass by, but help him.' (Ex 23:4-5) 'Balaam was riding on the donkey, and his two boys were with him. When the donkey saw the angel, she turned off the road, and went into a field. Then Balaam hit the donkey to make it go out on the road again. But the angel of Yahweh stood on a narrow lane between vineyards, with a stone wall on either side. When the donkey saw the angel of Yahweh, she shrank against the wall, crushing Balaam's foot against it, so he beat her again. Then Yahweh's angel went ahead, and stopped at a narrow place where there was no room to go either to the right or to the left. When the donkey saw Yahweh's angel there, she lay down under Balaam; he was angry, and beat her with a stick. But now Yahweh opened the mouth of the donkey, and she said to Balaam, "What have I done to you to make you beat me three times?"'(Num 22:22-27)

Sorry, dear reader, but I got carried away about Balaam and the donkey, and I must get back to the task in hand. This is Palm Sunday, a day of glory, of Hosannas, of olive branches, of triumph. My only reason for choosing to draw attention to the donkey is to highlight the reality of our own role in all of God's undertaking.

It is generally presumed that Mary may have travelled to Bethlehem, to Elizabeth's house, to Egypt, and back again, on the back of a donkey. It is also part of the Christmas story that there was a donkey in the stable at Bethlehem. Just before Jesus faced crucifixion and death, he was given a triumphant entry into Jerusalem on the back of a donkey. When I refer to our role as being somewhat like that of the donkey, what I'm saying is that the donkey is present, and is providing a service, but is not expecting or demanding any great plaudits or honours for doing so. Our vocation is one of service, whether that service is to God or to his people. The Hosanna of today were not for the donkey!

To do

'The greatest in the kingdom are those who serve', said Jesus, as he washed the feet of his apostles. This is one of the most beautiful secrets of the kingdom. The 'great' people in the world are those who lord it over others, and who have political, financial, or social clout. In God's kingdom, however, the greatest are the-basin-of-water-and-towel people. This is such a simple message that it's probably impossible to grasp! The gospels contain very simple messages for very complicated people. There is one idea that I need to clarify from the very start. From the moment of birth, a baby begins to show a unique personality. Some are born with a smile on their faces, and others enter this world with a howl, which lasts for many years. When I speak about being a person of service, I am not speaking of some sort of natural goodness or generosity; something that, for the one who has it, wouldn't be able to act with arrogance, or pride. What I speak of here is a pure gift of the Holy Spirit. That is what I need if I am to become a person of service; a donkey, always at the disposal of the Lord.

To say

Psalm 39

I said 'I will watch my ways, and keep my tongue from sin;
I will muzzle my mouth in front of the wicked.'
So I did. But as I kept silent, their happiness made my anguish grow.
My heart began to burn within, and when I could no longer contain my searing thoughts, I blurted out:
'Lord, let me know when my end will come;
let me know the number of my days; show me how frail and fleeting is my life.
You allow me live but a short span; before you, all my years are nothing.
Human existence is a mere whiff of breath.
Everyone is a mere shadow that goes about on earth.
Man is always in relentless pursuit, but all his labours lead to naught.
Doggedly he toils to rake in wealth, not knowing who will have it next.
But now, O Lord, what do I await? All my hope rests in you.

MONDAY IN HOLY WEEK

Pray

'Moses said to him "As soon as I leave the town, I will lift up my hands in prayer towards Yahweh, the thunder will cease, and there will be no more hail, and you will know that the earth is Yahweh's".' (Ex 9:29) 'The house of your servant David will be secure before you, because you, O Yahweh of Hosts, God of Israel, have made it known to your servant, and have said to him "Your family will last forever." This is why I have dared to address this prayer to you.' (2 Sam 7:27) 'Listen to the prayer and supplication of your servant, O Yahweh, my God; hearken to the cries and pleas which your servant directs to you today. Watch over this house of which you said, "My name shall rest there." Hear the prayer of your servant in this place.' (1 Kgs 8:28-29) 'If in the land of their exile, they come to themselves and repent, and they pray to you, saying "We have sinned. We confess how wicked and sinful we have been", hear from heaven, where your home is. Hear their prayer, be merciful to them, and forgive your people the sins they have committed against you.' (2 Chron 6:38-39) I will use no more quotes, even though I didn't get near what Jesus and the Letters have to say about prayer. What I have quoted should give some indication of just how seriously God's people took the whole question of prayer. They spoke to God as one who cared, as you who listened, as one who answered.

Prayer is a hunger within the human spirit. I am quite aware of the fact that our reflection for the first Monday of Lent was *Crying Out*, but prayer is such a broad and central part of our living, that there is little danger of much repetition here. We are into Holy Week, which is a time for quiet prayer, reflection, and waiting. It is a time of preparation, so that our hearts will be fully open to the wonders of the days ahead. Prayer is my lifeline with God. In this day and age most of us are familiar with sending messages all over the place at the touch of a button, whether on computer, mobile, or radio. If the connection is not *on*, and we are not in Prayer Mode, then our words fall to the ground and die.

To do

Prayer can be defined in many ways: Giving God time and space in my life; Working on my relationship with God; Sitting, waiting, and watching with the Lord. It matters not how we define it; what matters is that we pray. I hesitate to specify times, places, or methods here, because I believe that all of these will fall into place once the heart is open to prayer. There is no one method better than another, as long as we pray. Prayer is showing up, and the Spirit takes over from there. For example, if you agreed to take a few minutes out for prayer today, and 'nothing happens', then I can guarantee you that, if you keep doing this, you will be absorbed into prayer for longer and longer periods in no time at all. Prayer is what happens, when I show up. In other words, prayer is like love. Love is not a feeling, although it can often be accompanied by a feeling. Feelings don't last, however, and if my love for another is based on feelings alone, it is doomed. I have no control over feelings and, of themselves, they are neither right nor wrong. However, when love is a decision, then it becomes something that I can renew during every wakening hour. When it comes to prayer, as with many other things, Jesus asks for a decision, not a discussion! One of the surest ways of avoiding doing anything is to talk about it long enough!

To say

Psalm 1

Blessed is the man who never follows the counsel of the wicked,
Nor stands in the way of sinners, nor sits where the scoffers sit.
Instead he finds delight in the law of the Lord,
And meditates day and night on his commandments.
He is like a tree beside a brook,
Producing its fruit in due season, its leaves never withering.
Everything he does is a success.

TUESDAY IN HOLY WEEK

Penance

'Yahweh, the God of Israel says this: "The warning of this book shall not reach you, for your heart has been touched, and you have done penance in the presence of Yahweh, when you heard what I said against this place and its inhabitants".'(2 Kgs 22:19) 'If my people who bear my name humble themselves, do penance, and pray and look for me, and turn from their wicked ways, then I myself will hear from heaven, and forgive their sins, and restore their land.' (2 Chron 7:14) 'But when they were at peace, they did evil against you, and again you gave them over to the hands of the enemies, who oppressed them. Once more, they cried to you, repented and did penance, and you listened to them from heaven and, by your great kindness, you saved them many times.' (Neh 9:28) There is a fine line between repentance, penance, and sackcloth and ashes. I don't feel any great need to make a clear distinction between them, because they are part of the same journey back to God. For the purposes of today's reflection, however, I do need to say a few words about penance. For those of us who faced Ash Wednesday and Lent with gritted teeth, flexed muscles, and clenched fists, it may appear a bit late in the day to be speaking about penance. It's never too late for God, and better now than never.

Jesus had apostles, but he also had disciples. This word 'disciple' has something to do with living according to a certain discipline, or code of behaviour. To situate it properly, it is best to see it as connected to Calvary. After all, it is from that hill that rivers of grace flow that we call sacraments. St Paul speaks about us dying with Christ. In the ordinary course of loving others, I will often be called upon to die to myself – to my selfishness, my possessions, my opinions, my tiredness, etc. I may 'deprive' myself of some precious luxury, so that the money thus saved might feed a hungry child. Penance is part of Christian living whenever I am prepared to put the welfare of another before my own. Fasting, on occasions, can be most beneficial when the money thus saved goes to someone who has no food. Fasting is never an end in itself, except when it helps to control the appetites that can result from self-will run riot. St Paul speaks of disciplining the body, to bring it under subjection, so that the spirit and soul are strengthened through prayer. Self-control would be another word for penance. It is about proper balance between soul and body, which prevents the body taking control, to the detriment of the spirit. There is no end to the acts of penance any of us can do, and they can be of such a nature that they go totally unnoticed by others. Jesus condemned the Pharisees for making an outward show of penance, to gain the admiration and approval of others. The kingdom of God is built up in two ways: by tiny acts, most of which are hidden. To give some serious thought to this today is an ideal way to prepare for Good Friday. All of this is represented when I put a drop of water into the wine at the Offertory at Mass. This is my contribution, and it is made up of all the little 'dyings' that we all have to do in our living the Christian message.

To do

Once again, I hold back on the specifics, because we all are afforded many opportunities to perform small acts of penance, especially during this week. At the core of all of this is how I think of Calvary, and how that involves me. If I think of it as something that happened all those years ago, something from which we all now benefit, then I probably see no reason why there is anything that I can add through little acts of penance and self-discipline. St Paul saw it differently. 'I rejoice when I suffer for you; I complete in my own flesh what is lacking in the sufferings of Christ for the sake of his body, which is the church.' (Col 1:24) What he means is that he feels he can have a share in the sufferings of Jesus, so that he can become a greater instrument of blessing and new life to the church. In other words, I must be more than just a spectator on Calvary. I can enter into what happened there, and make it present wherever I am. Like the drop of water in the wine, my contribution is infinitesimal, but is none the less very real, very rewarding, and most blessed. What a privilege it is that through the simplest little acts of dying-to-self, I can actually share in the extraordinary and eternal events of Calvary.

To say

Psalm 15

O Lord, who will dwell in your tent, and reside on your holy mountain?
They who walk blamelessly and speak what is right,
Who speak truth from their hearts, and control their words;
Who look down on evildoers, but highly esteem God's servants;
Who at all costs stand by a pledged word;
Who do not lend money at interest, and refuses a bribe against the innocent.
They who do all this will never be shaken.

WEDNESDAY IN HOLY WEEK

Tears

'And it happened that a woman of this town, who was known as a sinner, heard that Jesus was in the Pharisee's house. She brought a precious jar of perfume, and stood behind him, at his feet, weeping. As she wet his feet with her tears, she dried them with her hair, and kissed his feet, and poured the perfume on them.' (Lk 7:37-38) 'You know how I lived among you, from the first day I set foot in the province of Asia, how I served the Lord in humility, through the tears and trials that the Jews caused me … Be on the watch, therefore, remembering that, for three years, night and day, I did not cease to warn everyone, even with tears.' (Acts 20:18-19, 31) 'Cry out to the Lord, O wall of the daughter of Zion! Oh, let your tears fall day and night, like rain. Give yourself no relief, grant your eyes no respite. Get up, cry out in the night, as the evening watches start; pour out your heart like water in the presence of the Lord. Lift up your hands to him for the lives of your children, who faint with hunger at the corner of every street.' (Lam 2:18) Once again I don't need to go further in scripture to where Jesus wept over Jerusalem, or at the tomb of Lazarus. Grief is the price we pay for love. If you don't want to cry at a funeral, then don't love anyone. When I chose the title *Tears* for this reflection, I was thinking more of the woman who washed Jesus' feet with her tears. Jesus said of her 'Her sins, her many sins, have been forgiven, because she has loved much.' There is something really beautiful and moving about this story. It reveals the depth of Jesus' love, and the extent of the sinner's brokenness. This woman actually risked her life when she did what she did. However, such was her need for forgiveness and acceptance, that it was a risk she was prepared to take. There is a hunger within the human heart, and when it is filled with the love of God, the tears can freely flow. The log-jam is broken, and love can flow again. What an extraordinary experience for her! How happy we all can feel for her. What a wonderful way to come to the Lord during this Holy Week. On Friday, as I kneel at the foot of the cross, when the drops of blood fall on my head, I can let my tears fall freely on the ground.

To do

I would strongly recommend to you, gentle reader, that you find time today, if possible, to read the whole story of this woman, which you will find in Luke's gospel, chapter 7, from verse 36 to the end of the chapter. Open your heart to the Spirit as you do this, and expect the tears to flow. They do not have to physically flow, but try to get a sense of release within as you pour out your love and thanks for such a wonderful unconditional love that is offered you by Jesus. This would be a good day, indeed, to receive the Sacrament of Reconciliation, unless your parish has a Reconciliation Service. This latter can be as personal as you choose to make it, even if you get to say very little. Jesus is more interested in what your heart is saying than anything you might wish to speak to him with your tongue.

To say

Psalm 77

I cry aloud to God – aloud that he may hear me.
In the day of trouble I seek the Lord,
And stretch out my hand untiringly, my soul refusing to be consoled.
When I think of God I sigh; when I meditate, my spirit fails.
I remember the deeds of the Lord; I recall his marvels of old.
I meditate on all your work, and consider your mighty deeds.
Your ways, O God, are most holy. Is there any god greater than you, our God?
You alone are the God who works wonders, who has displayed your power to all.

HOLY THURSDAY

Banquet

'If it pleases you, come with me to a banquet I have prepared for you.' (Esth 5:4) 'You prepare a banquet before me in the presence of my foes. You anoint my head with oil, my cup is overflowing.' (Ps 23:5) 'He has taken me to the banquet hall; his banner over me is love.' (Song 2:4) 'They are preparing a great banquet. They are spreading rugs for people to sit on. Everyone is eating and drinking.' (Is 21:5) 'On this mountain Yahweh Sabaoth will prepare for all the people a banquet of rich food and choice wines, meat full of marrow, fine wine strained.' (Is 25:6) 'So Jesus sent Peter and John, saying "Go and get everything ready for us to eat the Passover meal".' (Lk 22:8) 'You will eat and drink at my table in my kingdom.' (Lk 22:30) Banquets played an important part in the Jewish tradition. When God spoke to Moses, he commissioned him to make an offer to the people (who were really pagan at the time): *Tell them that I'll be their God, if they become my people. If they accept this, they must change their ways and, to give them guidelines on this, I will give them a set of Commandments. If they agree to this, then I ask that, once a year, they come together to share a meal, during which they will remember this covenant, and all I have done for them.* It was during such a meal that Jesus brought this to its completion with an extraordinary announcement: *My Father will be your Father too, if you are willing to become like little children. To help you in this, you are given just two Commandments, about loving God, and loving each other. If you accept this, I will leave you with a special meal, when I will continue to be with you, and we will celebrate this new and eternal covenant.*

This Last Supper Banquet is the very summit of God's sharing with his people, when he invites us to sit at table with him, to share his own Son with us. 'For God loved the world so much that he sent his only Son, so that they who believe in him would have eternal life.' (Jn 3:16)

To do

This is a wonderful day, and I hope you get an opportunity to share in the church ceremonies of this evening. This is love and service of the highest possible level being enjoyed and celebrated by God's people. If you have time, I would strongly suggest that you read chapters 13 to 17 of St John's gospel. It is the night before his death, and Jesus is leaving them with a powerful legacy. His teachings about love, service, the Holy Spirit, and his resurrection are a must for all of us to read. Let me put it to you this way. A young doctor discovered that he had terminal cancer, and it was of such a nature that he knew he had very little time left. He had a young family, and it was breaking his heart, because he had always fantasised being there for them at every step of the way as they grew up. He would advise them, listen to them, encourage them. Now he was being robbed of all that. In desperation, he got a few C90 cassettes, and he poured out his heart in those. He told his children how much he loved them, how he would always be there for them, what he hoped for them, etc. Some years after his death, when they were a bit older, his wife allowed the kids listen to the tapes. Each was supplied with personal copies. Over the next twenty years or so those tapes were listened to again and again. They helped guide the kids through their most difficult years. I liken Chapters 13 to 17 of John's gospel to tapes that Jesus left us the night before he died. But then, of course, he came back … and he also sent the Spirit to remind us.

To say

Psalm 40

Blessed is the man who relies on the Lord,
And does not look to the proud or go astray after false gods.
How numerous, O Lord, are your wonderful deeds!
In your marvellous plans for us you are beyond compare.
How many there are – I cannot tell them, or count their number.
Sacrifice and oblation you do not desire; but you have given me an open heart.
Burnt offerings and sin offerings you do not require.
Then I said 'Here I am, as the scroll says of me.
To do your will is my delight, O God, for your law is within my heart.'
In the congregation I have proclaimed the good news of salvation.
My lips, O Lord, I do not seal – you know that very well.

GOOD FRIDAY

Staying

'And he said to them "My soul is filled with sorrow even to death. Remain here with me, and stay awake".'(Mt 26:38) 'But you have been with me, and stood by me through all my troubles.' (Lk 22:28) 'As they drew near the village they were heading for, Jesus made as if to go on further. But they prevailed upon him: "Stay with us, for night comes quickly. The day is now almost over." So he went in to stay with them.' (Lk 24:28-29) 'And John also gave this testimony: "I saw the Spirit coming down upon him like a dove from heaven, and it stayed with him".' (Jn 1:32) 'So, when they came to him, they asked him to stay with them, and Jesus stayed there two days.' (Jn 4:40) 'They did not stay with us, because they did not really belong to us. Had they belonged to us, they would have stayed with us.' (1 Jn 2:19) On a day like today I could have chosen many titles for a reflection, and yet *Staying* was the one that came to mind. I believe my reason for this was something along the following lines: When I was a child, I was quite convinced that if Mary and Joseph had come to my door on that first Christmas night, I would certainly have welcomed them, and brought them in. I also was convinced that, if I had been on Calvary, I would not have run away, but would have stood right there with Mary all through the ordeal. Alas, for my innocence! Life has shown me just how selective I can be, when it comes to standing under crosses! I can turn down side streets, or look up at the sky when I see certain people approaching! There are others, and I wouldn't dare ask them how they are, in case they'd tell me!

No, I was not on Calvary; but I can be there any day I choose.. Calvary was Jesus saying *Yes* to the Father, and this was the antidote for the *No* of Original Sin. Every time I offer Eucharist, I can join my yes to Jesus, to his yes to the Father. As I pray the Divine Mercy Chaplet, I can stand with Mary on Calvary, and pray, 'For the sake of his most sorrowful passion, have mercy on us, and on the whole world.' I am part of a church that is on Calvary at the moment. Every time I watch pope John Paul II struggle to take a step, or utter a word, I realise that he, too, is on Calvary. St Padre Pio spent his life on Calvary. As I stand with Mary at the foot of the cross she reassures me that all will be well, and that Easter is only around the corner. The only real sin I can commit, as a Christian, is not to have hope.

To do

I can make Calvary the very centre and core of my spirituality. In my prayer I can stand at the foot of the cross, as the drops of blood fall on my head, and seep through my whole system. I can relive Calvary every time I approach the altar to celebrate Eucharist. I can place the Divine Mercy message right at the centre of my spiritual life. When I sit in the Divine Presence, I can do so as if I were standing with Mary on Calvary. By doing this, the whole gospels come alive for me. Despite my childhood fantasies, I probably would have run away, had I lived back then. I have a choice today, however, and I can choose to remain at the foot of the cross. The body of Christ still hangs from a cross in many parts of today's world. Any concern, empathy, or compassion I have for the down-trodden, marginalized, or repressed peoples of this world can become part of my vigil at the foot of the cross. Take Calvary out of the picture, and the whole centre falls out of my life as a Christian.

To say

Psalm 22

My God, my God, why have you forsaken me?
Why are you so far from me, from the sound of my groaning?
But I am a worm, and not a man, scorned by men, despised by people.
All who see me make a jest of me; they sneer and shake their heads.
'He put his trust in the Lord, let the Lord rescue him! If the Lord is his friend, let him help him!'

* * *

All you who fear the Lord praise him! All you sons of Jacob glorify him! All you sons of Israel revere him!
For he has not scorned or loathed the afflicted in his misery.
He has not hidden his face from him, but has listened when he cried to him.
The whole earth from end to end will remember and turn to the Lord; the pagan nations will worship him.
For dominion belongs to the Lord, and he reigns over the nations.

HOLY SATURDAY

Waiting

'But these things I plan won't happen right away. Slowly, steadily, surely, the time approaches when the vision will be fulfilled. If it seems slow, wait patiently, for it will surely take place. It will not be delayed.' (Hab 2:3) 'As for me, I will watch expectantly for Yahweh, waiting hopefully for the God who saves me.' (Mic 7:7) 'Those who wait for me will never be put to shame.' (Is 49:23) 'Keep calm before the Lord, wait for him in patience.' (Ps 37:7) 'I wait for your deliverance, Lord.' (Gen 49:18) If I walk into a church today, there are certain things I expect to see: the altar is bare, the tabernacle is empty; all flowers and candles are removed, and all statues covered. There is a sense of emptiness about the place. This helps heighten the emphasis on waiting, on some sort of in-between time, when nothing is happening. This must have been a long day for the apostles, at least for those among them who did believe that he would come back to them. It must have been a day of quiet prayer and hope for Mary. She was used to waiting. She had waited for Bethlehem, and she would later have to encourage the apostles to wait for Pentecost.

In the severe pain of bereavement, it's not easy to think about the whole idea of waiting. That will come in time; but, for now, all that is present is the sharp and painful sense of loss. Quite a lot of things can happen when we are totally unaware of anything happening. The Spirit works that way. I walked past where there had been a gorse fire on the mountains some months previously, and, as I used a stick to poke through the black ash, I was amazed to discover a whole new growth of green grass emerging underneath. While we know that this will happen, we may not see any evidence of that fact. This focus is much sharper when it comes to the workings of God. That is why I said in yesterday's reflection that the only real sin I can commit, as a Christian, is not to have hope.

To do

Not everything stops on Holy Saturday! It is a wonderful day for reflection and prayer. There is so much to reflect on, and to pray about. This story has to do with our death and resurrection also. There is a sense of gestation about this day, as we await the celebration of new life. We wait with that sure and certain hope referred to in the letter to the Hebrews. Apart from today, we have many such moments in our lives, when we have no choice but to wait, hope, and pray. Today resembles what it might have been like before Creation. There is a void, and it is about to be filled. Once life begins it never ends, as it moves through the various stages into the eternal ocean. I remember a niece of mine, at about four years of age, asking her mam, 'Is this a nothing day, mammy?' She clapped her hands with delight when she was told that it was. My sister explained that the child went to playschool Monday to Friday, and to Mass on Sunday, so Saturday was a 'nothing day'! How are you going to use your nothing day?

To say

Psalm 40

With resolve I waited for the Lord; he listened and heard me beg.
Out of the horrid pit he drew me, out of the quagmire in the bog.
He settled my feet upon a rock, and made my steps steady.
He put a new song in my mouth, a song of praise to our God.
Many will see and be awed, and put their trust in the Lord.
How numerous, O Lord, are your wonderful deeds!
In your marvellous plans for us you are beyond compare.
How many they are – I cannot tell them or count their number.
In the congregation I have proclaimed the good news of salvation.
I have not merely kept within my heart your saving help, but have spoken about it.

EASTER SUNDAY

Alleluia!

'When our perishable being puts on imperishable life, when our mortal being puts on immortality, the word of scripture will be fulfilled: "Death has been swallowed up by victory. Death, where is your victory? Death, where is your sting?"' (1 Cor 15:54-55) 'The time of my victory is near, and my victory will be final.' (Is 51:5-6) 'The horses are prepared for battle, but the victory belongs to the Lord.' (Prov 21:31) 'Yahweh, no one but you can stand up for the powerless against the powerful. Come to our help, Yahweh our God. We rely on you, and fight against this huge army in your name. Yahweh, you are our God, and in you is our victory.' (2 Chron 14:10) This is the day that the Lord has made; let us rejoice and be glad in it. Jesus has overcome the final enemy, death, and the field is filled with good wheat again. We are truly privileged in that we can share in Christ's life, his death, and his victory. Dying, you destroyed our death; rising, you restored our life. Lord Jesus, come in glory. By your cross and resurrection you have set us free. You are the Saviour of the world. The candles are lit again, the bells are ringing, and the songs of joy fill the church. Because of God's plan for us, this is our victory also, and we have good reason to celebrate. St Paul writes: 'Since you have been raised to new life with Christ, set your sights on the realities of heaven, where Christ sits at God's right hand, in the place of honour and power. Let heaven fill your thoughts. Do not think only about things down here on earth. For you died when Christ died, and your real life is hidden with Christ in God. And when Christ, who is your real life, is revealed to the whole world, you will share in all his glory.' (Col 3:1-4)

To do

I rejoice in this day; of course I do. But I must remember that, for me, the victory is not yet complete. On the evening of the resurrection, if the pressure came on, the apostles probably would have run away again. They had to wait for their Easter, which we call Pentecost. On Easter morning, the stone was rolled away, and Jesus came out into new life. On Pentecost morning, the doors of the Upper Room were flung open, and the apostles came out completely transformed, ready to go forth to witness to the resurrection, and to do so at the cost of their own lives. The mission entrusted to them was to witness to Christ's resurrection. This was the good news entrusted to them, and they were to spread that across the face of the earth. 'Go and tell my disciples that I have risen' was the message Jesus entrusted to Mary Magdalene. (Jn 20:17) This mission is also our mission. If I am willing to experience dying within myself, I will certainly experience resurrection. The greatest witness a recovering alcoholic can give is to walk down the main street of his home town sober. It is only when we ourselves experience resurrection, experience the victory in our own lives, that we can give witness to that fact to others. You can be a life-giving person, if you choose to. This is a good day to decide.

To say

Psalm 9

I will thank you, Lord, with all my heart; I will tell of all the marvellous things you have done.
I will be filled with joy because of you. I will sing praises to your name, O Most High.
My enemies turn away in retreat; they are overthrown and destroyed before you.
For you have judged in my favour; from your throne, you have judged in fairness.
The Lord reigns forever, executing judgement from his throne.
He will judge the world with justice, and rule the nations with fairness.
Sing praises to God who reigns in Jerusalem.
Tell the world about his unforgettable deeds.